"As a new Future of Work is being shaped before our eyes, we're seeing a shift of power. Instead of working for an organisation, employees are increasingly organisation, using it as a platform for realising their personal purpose. *Enter* fabulously creative and engaging handbook for the purpose hungry intrapren activist, who aspires to change the world by changing their relationship to wor

– **Gib Bulloch**, Author, *The Intrapreneur: Confessions of a Corporate Insurgent*

"There are many books on how to improve your relationships with your partners, parents, children … heck, even with yourself. Have you ever wondered about how you relate to your work? Not just on a love or hate spectrum, but really, deep down? Chances are you haven't. Until now!

Enter Your Flow takes you on an exciting journey of self-discovery about every aspect of your relationship with your work and your career. You'll be guided to become aware of your choices so that you can take the driver's seat and make conscious decisions about what you want your job to be, who you want to work with, and what ignites your inner spark.

Chapter after chapter you will feel more and more immersed in this fantastic journey of self-discovery, and you will have the best guides and travel companions to show you all the sights to see. Bon voyage!"

– **Dr. Julia Furedi**, Organizational Psychologist, Author and Founder: sparq

"This book will be a friend and guide to you as you explore yourself and take charge of building your own career. Lots of fun and inspiring hands-on examples help you turn your ideas into action. And if other colleagues and friends are ready to join you on your work-life journey – get ready and enter the flow together."

– **Gabriele Zedlmayer**, Special Advisor, International Affairs, University of the People

"If you consider reading *Enter Your Flow*, don't waste time deciding. Just get it and enjoy how this book can transform your life. I have encountered thousands of professionals asking themselves how to create a more fulfilling and purpose-driven way to work. Finally, with *Enter Your Flow* there's a book that provides the pathway to get there. Like a personal coach, the authors provide step-by-step guidance for creating the life we're meant to live. And the illustrations simply make this book a fun and human-centric journey all around."

– **Peter Matthies**, Founder of the Conscious Business Institute

“This book beams with hope and informed optimism about anyone’s potential to ‘become who you might have been’ (in the words of George Eliot). It provides an engaging set of practical tools and exercises to take you through your personal journey to discover your ‘flow channel’. Whether you’re looking for ways to be more creative and authentically ‘you’ in your current job or are searching for fulfillment of your potential in life in general, you’ll find great support and inspiration here. The authors share generously from their own personal experiences. In addition, they share stories of other people who have been at a similar juncture and made it through to a happier place – a place, where ‘flow’ is the new normal, and work is fun, rewarding and meaningful. It’s the kind of book you’ll keep coming back to as you practice your ‘flow’ – I will for sure!”

– **Louise Agersnap**, innovation expert, social scientist and artist

“This book is a wonderful guide on the journey to a fulfilling career and life. Well done to the authors for designing a flow with exercises that stimulate both the right and left brains to find our unique “Me Magic”! ”

– **Valerie Abrellduong**, International Committee of the Red Cross

Enter your Flow

AN INTERACTIVE JOURNEY TOWARD
FULFILLMENT AND HAPPINESS IN YOUR WORK LIFE

TONY ANAGOR
ZSUZSANNA FERENCZI
PAUL JEREMAES
JOHN ZIMMER
Illustrations
KEVIN WOODSON

Hasmark™
PUBLISHING
INTERNATIONAL

Published by Hasmark Publishing
www.hasmarkpublishing.com

First Edition

Disclaimer

This book is based on our knowledge, experience, and opinions. It was written to provide information and motivation to our readers. The methods described in this book are not intended to be a definitive set of instructions. The advice and strategies contained herein might not be suitable for your situation. You might discover other methods and materials to achieve the same result. You should consult with a professional where appropriate. No warranties or guarantees are expressed or implied by the inclusion of any of the content in this book. Neither the publisher nor the individual authors shall be liable for any physical, psychological, emotional, financial, or commercial damages.

Editor: Stephen Buffey
stephen@hasmarkpublishing.com

Cover Designer:Anne Karklins
anne@hasmarkpublishing.com

Interior Layout: Kevin Woodson, Anne Karklins

ISBN 13: 978-1-77482-194-7
ISBN 10: 177482194X

Hasmark PUBLISHING INTERNATIONAL

We dedicate this book to everyone who has helped us move forward on our own journeys—family, friends, colleagues. It is impossible to measure the impact that your support, guidance, and love have had on us.

We also dedicate this book to everyone who has taken up the challenge to embark upon their own journey toward a fulfilling and rewarding work life.

Table of Contents

INTRODUCTION

Your Journey Begins Here

"Your work is going to fill a large part of your life, and the only way to be truly satisfied is to do what you believe is great work. And the only way to do great work is to love what you do."
– Steve Jobs

A question

Why did you pick up this book?

There are hundreds of other things that you could be doing right now. Things that demand your attention at this very moment. Work obligations and personal obligations.

And yet, here you are.

Reading.

Why? What will your reward be for continuing? What will you get in exchange for the time that you spend with this book?

The answer depends on you.

A journey

We invite you to embark on a journey.

A journey to understand your relationship with, and approach to, work.

A journey to create a more fulfilling and happier work life.

The word "work," has several connotations, many of which, unfortunately, are negative. We might think of work from the perspective of the mental or physical effort that is required to do a task. We might think of it as an obligation from Monday morning until Friday afternoon. We might think of it as a necessary trade-off for the money that we are paid until the day when we can finally retire.

Alternatively, if we think of work as the foundation of a fulfilling career or vocation, it takes on a different meaning. It is something that we look forward to doing; it excites us and motivates us. Mondays are just as enjoyable as any other day of the week, perhaps even more so.

The purpose that you identify with your work can provide a level of fulfillment that makes the work worthwhile. In many cases, your attitude towards work will depend on the story that you tell yourself about the reasons why you do what you do.

The average person will spend more than ninety thousand hours at work over the course of their lifetime. That time amounts to approximately 25% of an average lifespan. No matter how you look at your work, that is a significant amount of your time. When you consider that you also spend about 33% of your life sleeping, the importance of your attitude towards work comes into even sharper focus.

As you explore this book, you will discover that there is much more to be gained from your relationship to work than the products or services that you provide or the salary that you earn. Your interpretation of, and relationship to, your work is tremendously important.

Developing a clearer understanding of what satisfaction and success mean to you in relation to your work will allow you to chart a course that leads to rewarding destinations, and that also allows you to enjoy the journey. When you embark on this journey, you will truly be able to enter your flow and achieve a heightened sense of fulfillment and happiness in your work life.

How you experience your journey is up to you. The fulfillment that you feel and the rewards that you reap will be unique. After all, you know better than anyone what is important to you. However, you will not embark on this journey alone, there will be help along the way.

You will get help within the pages of this book, but we are not so presumptuous as to think that we have all the answers. As you progress along your journey, help will also arrive from different sources: from the people around you; from other materials that you read; from the things that you see; from the things that you do. It will sometimes come from unexpected sources, and it will also come from within you.

Why we wrote this book

We came together to write this book from different vantage points. Collectively, we have more than one hundred years of work experience in different industries, in the private and public sectors. What we have experienced in our own careers has not been achieved without getting a few battle scars along the way.

When we brought our experiences together, we realized that the lessons and insights that we had accumulated were too important to be left untold. Thus, we set out on a journey of our own by coming together. We wanted to uncover the elements that lead to a happy, successful, and satisfying work life. As with many things in life, we often found that the secrets were hidden in plain sight.

Initially, these elements might seem obvious and easy to implement in your own life. The reality, however, is that many people become trapped in a downward spiral of work pressures, poor leadership and directives, bad work environments, colleagues who are struggling to find their own way, and even societal pressures. When left unchecked, this downward spiral results in talents, creativity, and values becoming diluted or, even worse, erased.

Fortunately, this does not have to be your reality. Nor does it require a reactionary response to survive. Instead, it is possible to build inner strength and clarify who you are, the unique value that you bring to the work that you do, and the satisfaction that you derive from it. We want to accompany you on this journey.

We are not promising that it will always be easy; no journey ever is.

You might find this book challenging to read. Some parts might make you feel uncomfortable. That is not a bad thing; the greatest personal growth comes from situations in which we are pushed outside of our comfort zone. As the American President Franklin Roosevelt said, "A smooth sea never made a skilled sailor."

We are asking you to challenge yourself to reflect on who you are, why you are doing the work that you do and what, if anything, you would like to change.

Our hope is that by helping you gain clarity in your approach to work, your personal journey will be enriched, and you will be able to reach your full potential. More than this, we want you to share and articulate your experiences in a way that creates a positive impact in the lives of others, and ultimately, your workplace.

What this book is (and is not)

This book is not a "how-to" book in the traditional sense of business books. We offer no advice when it comes to preparing your CV or creating your LinkedIn profile. We do not offer any tips on how to conduct a job search or prepare for an interview. There are plenty of excellent resources out there that deal with these matters, and we encourage you to investigate and use them as necessary.

This book is about something deeper. This book is about *you*.

The structure of this book

The book is divided into three parts to help you navigate your journey. We have called these parts *Frame*, *Focus*, and *Flow*. Each has a different objective.

Frame

The first part of the book will help you to take stock of where you are now and frame your current work situation. You will reflect on who you are and how connected you are to the work that you do. You will spend time thinking about the organization for which you work and the people with whom you work. Finally, you will reflect on the things that motivate you at work and how they relate to your personal values.

By having a clear understanding of the frame within which you are currently working, you will establish the foundation upon which you can discover, explore, and develop new insights into your full potential.

Focus

The second part of the book invites you to focus on your strengths, your aspirations, and your development areas. You will think about the things that you love to do, why you love to do them, and how you can do them more often or better. You will also come face-to-face with any limiting beliefs that you might have about yourself and how you can start to change and overcome those beliefs.

As you focus more deeply on your unique talents, you will also explore your capacity for creativity and innovation. You will unlock new insights into the conditions that you require to bring out your best and derive greater satisfaction from the things that you do.

This focus will enable you to chart a course to reach your full potential through self-development and growth. It might lead to a new job or career, or it might lead to making some changes where you already are. As Liam Neeson's character Qui-Gon Jinn tells Anakin Skywalker in the film *Star Wars: Episode I – The Phantom Menace*, "Your focus determines your reality."

Flow

The final part of the book will help you transform your newly enhanced vision into reality and enter your personal flow channel. You will use your insights, confidence, and resilience to find your voice. With a deeper awareness of your aspirations, motivation, and personal values, you will have the confidence to speak out authentically with your unique voice.

However, speaking out about the things that are important to you is not enough; you must act if you want fulfillment and happiness in your work life. That means making some decisions. You will explore the decision-making process and how your flow channel can help guide the decisions that you make.

You are also the author

If you are serious about embarking on this journey, you should be prepared to do so in an open-minded and thoughtful manner. As you will soon discover, this is not the type of book that you simply read from cover to cover. It is much more interactive than that.

There will be questions for you to answer and exercises for you to complete. From time to time, we will ask you to stop for personal reflection. Occasionally you will be asked to go back and revisit previous parts of the book with a new perspective. It is all part of the process to help you expand your thinking and uncover new insights into your relationship with your work.

Because such a journey requires both left- and right-brain thinking, this book combines text with an interactive, illustrated narrative. The illustrations are an integral part of the reading experience. In an era where visual communication is commonplace, we take this concept one step further, and invite you to:

Be inspired

Record

Explore

In a very real way, you are the co-author of this book. When you reach the final page, you will have engaged with the content in a unique way and transformed the book into something far more valuable than what it was when you first picked it up. This book, as modified and supplemented with your notes, insights, and reflections, will become your personal, one-of-a-kind "Journey Map" and it will provide the foundation for the long-term development of your purpose-driven career journey.

Aye aye, Captain!

You are the captain of the ship that is your life. Sometimes the waters will be calm and sometimes they will be stormy, but you should be the one who decides in which direction the ship will go. If not you, then who?

During his years of imprisonment on Robben Island, Nelson Mandela found strength in the poem "Invictus" written in 1875 by William Ernest Henley. The final stanza of that poem reads:

> *It matters not how strait the gate,*
>
> *How charged with punishments the scroll,*
>
> *I am the master of my fate,*
>
> *I am the captain of my soul.*

We want you to enjoy each discovery along your journey and to have the satisfaction that comes from making a meaningful and lasting impact in your work life.

Are you ready? If so, turn the page and prepare to set sail!

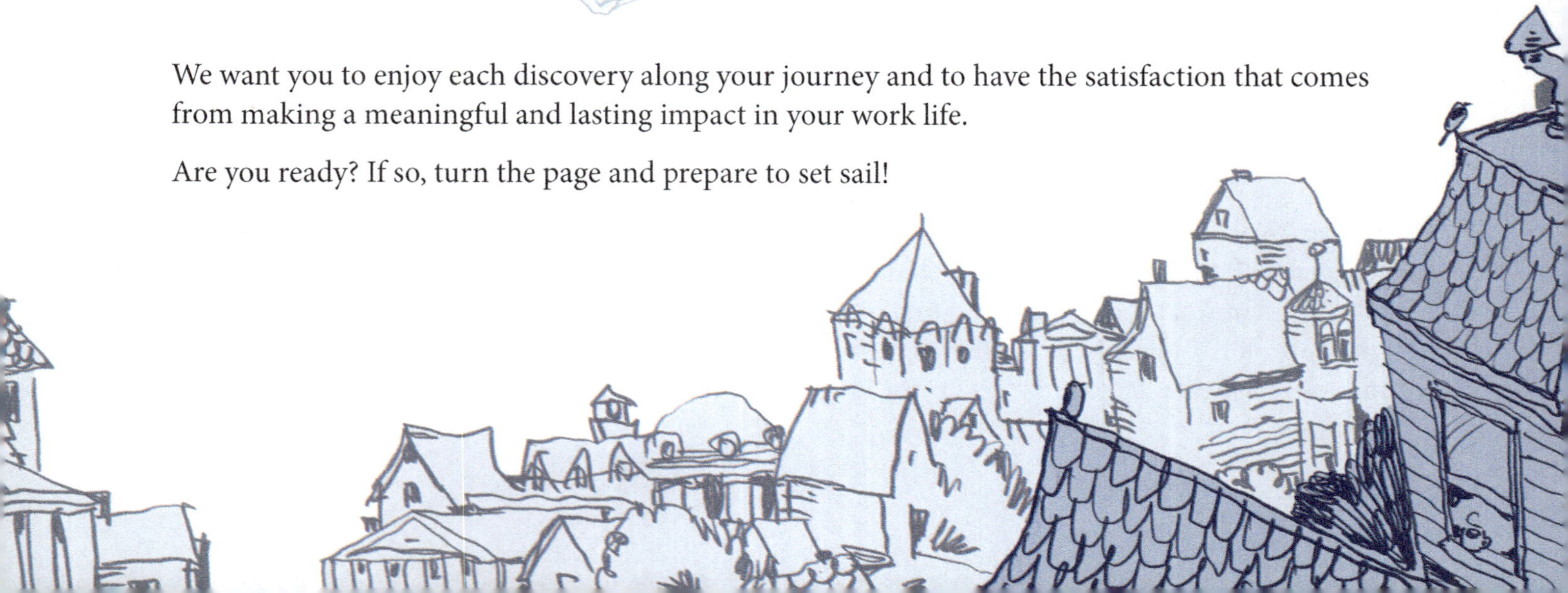

PART ONE

FRAME

CHAPTER ONE

Bringing Me to Work

"There is no such thing as work-life balance – it is all life.
The balance has to be within you."
– Sadhguru

A cast of thousands

Think about your most recent workday. Perhaps it was yesterday, perhaps it was a few days ago. What was it like?

When did it start and when did it end? Where were you and with whom did you interact? What did you do all day? Was it a good day, a bad day or an average day? How did you feel when you went to bed?

Put the book down, close your eyes and walk through that day in as much detail as possible in your mind, paying particular attention to how you felt.

Now, let's flip the lens in the other direction. Think about your next workday. Perhaps it will be tomorrow; perhaps it will be in a few days. Do you have anything planned? Where will you be and what will you do? Are you looking forward to it? Are you looking forward to interacting with people?

Once again, put the book down, close your eyes and in your mind, imagine your day unfolding the way that you expect it will. How does it make you feel?

You have now reflected on two workdays … out of the more than ten thousand that you will likely have in your life. Are you happy with how things are going?

A wake-up call

When the alarm clock rings, it is time for you to get up. You start to get ready for work following your usual weekday routine. Whether you are going to the office or settling down to work from home, you probably have the same ritual every day. That ritual certainly includes at least some of the following: exercise; shower; dress; breakfast; keys; wallet; purse; smartphone. You finally sit down at your desk, open your laptop and are ready to work.

The question is, are you *fully* bringing yourself to work?

You might say, "That's a strange question. Of course, I am fully bringing myself to work! Where else am I?"

In our experience, the answer is not as obvious as one might think. The key word in the question is "fully." Did you fully bring yourself to work? Is your mind in it? Is your heart in it? Is your energy in it? Are you truly present, giving the best of yourself with 100% focus on the tasks at hand? Can you imagine what being 100% present and focused would feel like?

Now, let's be clear. You do have to show up physically, whether in person or online. If you don't, that will not work for very long (and neither will you). But bringing yourself to work is about more than physically showing up and sitting your butt down in a chair.

Much more.

Crazy little thing called "work"

In 1979, the legendary rock band Queen released their hit "Crazy Little Thing Called Love." Many people feel that, on most days, they have to deal with a crazy little thing called work. It is understandable.

Here are a few scenarios we have lived through in our lives. In each case, we were not fully bringing ourselves to work. Of course, one can experience many, or all, of these scenarios over the course of one's career. It is almost never the same scenario from beginning to end. Do you recognize yourself in any of them?

Cog

Nine o'clock sharp: maybe you are at your desk and going through email.

Ten o'clock: perhaps you have a team meeting.

Half past twelve: lunch with a colleague.

Half past one: back at your desk.

Three o'clock: time for coffee(s).

Five o'clock (or six o'clock or seven o'clock?): shut down the computer and head home or, perhaps, out for a drink with friends or colleagues.

Whatever your routine, do you put up with it because, well, that is the way it has always been, and you never wondered whether it could be different? Perhaps you felt that there was no other option.

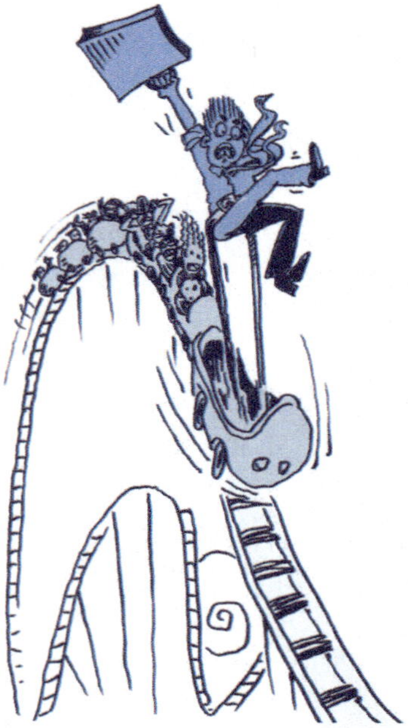

Roller-coaster

At times, do you feel challenged and stimulated? The work is exciting, and you ride the opportunity while it lasts, which gives you personal and professional satisfaction. But eventually, the moment always passes. The positive energy fades and you are back to the bottom of the roller coaster looking at a steep climb in front of you.

Responsibility

You keep going because you feel responsible for the people with whom you work. You owe it to your boss, your teammates, and your other colleagues. You tell yourself that you have to show up for them.

Drag

Do you feel that going to work is a struggle? You almost need to drag yourself into the office. You are driven by the constant pressure to meet the expectations of your boss, your clients or other stakeholders. Have you, knowingly or unknowingly, created rules which oblige you to keep working? Rules about authority; rules about self-respect; rules about financial security.

Gilded Cage

Perhaps you earn a good salary and other benefits that come with the job. They certainly help to dull the nagging discomfort that you feel, and of course you deserve to be paid fairly for the work that you do.

But, ultimately, is it a fair trade? Should work mean something more?

Time waits for no one

As these feelings keep you in check, you continue to work and the years pass. Time waits for no one.

We understand that this can make for bleak reading, but it is important to be honest. As is the case with any bad situation, you must acknowledge it and understand it before you can change it.

According to Gallup's 2021 *State of the Workplace* report, employee engagement decreased globally from 22% in 2019 to 20% in 2020. That was actually an improvement since 2009 when employee engagement was a shocking 12%! Meanwhile, stress and burnout have risen sharply, exacerbated by the COVID-19 pandemic.

When it comes to work, far too many people are either not fully engaged or completely disengaged. Several recent surveys have found that anywhere from 50% to 67% of workers would choose a different career if they could start again. One of the top regrets that people have about their careers is that they wish that they had quit a particular job sooner.

And then there is the phenomenon which has been around for a long time, but which gained such traction in 2022 that it has been given a name: quiet quitting. When someone engages in quiet quitting, they do not leave their job. They do the minimum that is required of them and no more. Many quiet quitters are not actively engaged at work and all of them draw a hard boundary between their work life and their private life: no checking emails outside of work hours and no putting in extra time after 5:00 p.m.

It does not have to be this way. Spending 90,000 hours of your life in a negative situation is not a great way to spend your time.

There is an alternative. You can, and should, do better.

The meaning of work

When you feel that you are doing meaningful work, you are fully engaged and connected to what you do. You wake up every morning looking forward to what the day will bring. You can be yourself and you are in sync with your values.

You bring your heart and mind to the workplace and are passionate about what you do. You are committed to your organization, your colleagues, and your clients. You put effort into everything you do. You make an impact and receive recognition for what you do.

Of course, there are challenges along the way and some days are more stressful than others. But the stress is mainly eustress, the positive form of stress. Examples include being asked to take the lead on a major client

presentation or organizing a big office event. It is a stress that brings growth and opportunities. You feel tired at the end of the day, but it is the tiredness that comes with the satisfaction of having done a good day's work.

In simple terms, you are engaged. You feel that you belong, that people care about you, and that you are working for a worthy purpose.

> Work is fun.
>
> Work is rewarding.
>
> Work is meaningful.

During the writing of this book, we asked many people the following question: When you have had a great day at work, what happened that made it a great day?

We put this question to people who were at the beginning of their careers as well as those with several years of experience. They were people in large and small companies in various industries. They were people in a wide variety of positions within their respective companies.

Each person responded in his or her own way, but we noticed a common theme that can best be summarized as follows:

> *A great day is one in which I made a difference for someone. I provided value or solved a problem. I felt good about myself and what I had done. It mattered.*

What can we do to ensure that this feeling is not a rare event, but rather something that we experience almost every day?

EXERCISE: How do you show up at work?

When you think of your relationship to work, are you fully showing up? What goes through your mind as the days pass? Don't just think of one day in particular; you cannot judge your overall engagement and connection to your work based on one day. Have a broader perspective that takes the entire experience at your organization into account—good times, bad times, and ordinary times.

Put the book down and think about it.

Now that you have reflected, we have some statements that we would like you to read and score. For each of these statements, rate them on a scale of 1–10 where 1 means that you disagree completely and 10 means that you agree completely.

One more thing: there is no number 7. That is not a mistake. You cannot choose 7. It is far too often the "safe choice" when rating something on a scale of 1–10. Removing the number 7 forces people to do some deeper thinking.

STATEMENTS

I am having the time of my life.

1 2 3 4 5 6 8 9 10

I use my strengths and make a meaningful contribution.

1 2 3 4 5 6 8 9 10

I feel connected and can show up as myself.

1 2 3 4 5 6 8 9 10

I am rewarded and recognized for my work.

1 2 3 4 5 6 8 9 10

I understand the company's vision and my future in it.

1 2 3 4 5 6 8 9 10

Add up the points for the five statements. Now, multiply that number by 2 to get a score out of 100. For example, if someone scored 5, 6, 4, 9 and 6, the total would be 30. Multiplying that by 2 would yield a score of 60 out of 100.

Are you happy with your total score? Are you happy with the scores in response to each of the five statements? For example, you could score 10 on four of the statements and 1 on the remaining statement. That would yield a total score of 82 out of 100. While this might seem good on the surface, if you consistently score low on one of the statements, eventually it will have an impact on how you feel at work.

Rating the five statements above will help you take stock of how you are feeling at work right now. The exercise is a good insight into the pillars of your work life.

The pillars of your work life

Your career is built on pillars, and it is the strength of those pillars that will determine the amount of satisfaction that you derive from the work that you do.

In our experience, people feel most satisfied with their work when it is built on a solid foundation. The five pillars of this foundation are passion, contribution, psychological safety, reward and recognition, and a promising future.

Let's look at each of them in turn.

The First Pillar: Passion

Passion brings out happiness and excitement. Passion makes it possible for you to feel successful and fulfilled at work. Passion allows you to advance in your career and ultimately to live a better life.

When you are passionate about what you do, you understand the importance of your role in relation to the direction and purpose of your organization. You see a meaningful connection between yourself, your contributions, and the organization where you work.

Out of the lab and into the forest

Jason was a researcher at a large tech company. While he was good at what he was doing, he was not comfortable with the work. The research lab where Jason worked was part of a huge campus, built on old farmland with a lot of fields and forests around the buildings.

As time passed, Jason became more and more interested in the wildlife and the environment of the campus. Eventually, he was spending more time outside than he was spending in the lab. Management saw that Jason felt disconnected with the research that he was doing. So, they worked with him to find a job that suited him better

Eventually, Jason became a facility site manager. Part of his new job was to look after the environment and the wildlife. For the first time in a long time, he felt passion for what he was doing and put all his energy into his work.

The organization accepted Jason for who he was and understood that his passion could lead to opportunities for himself and the company.

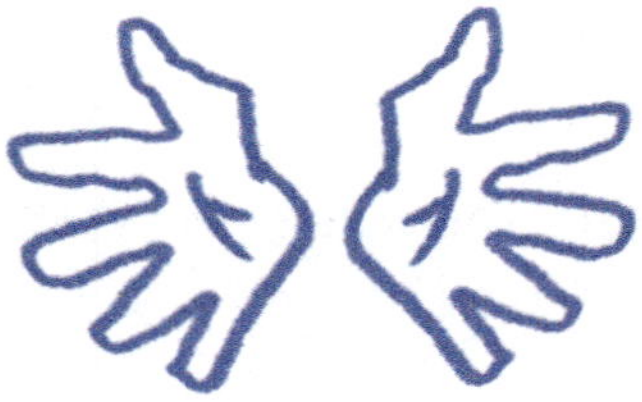

The Second Pillar: Contribution

When you believe that you are making a meaningful contribution at work, you feel more connected to the work that you do. It starts with understanding your strengths. When you can match what you love doing with what you are good at, you do your best work. It feels natural. You feel at ease even when you are being stretched.

As a result, through your personal growth, you get better at what you do and have a greater chance of standing out and being recognized for your unique capabilities. This in turn brings more energy and motivation.

Author's story

At each stage of Paul's career there has been cumulative development, personal discovery, and enhancement to the contributions that he has been able to make. The same is true of the satisfaction and success that he derived from those contributions.

Paul's early beginnings as a musician and telecommunications engineer naturally opened opportunities over the years for him to deliver value as a computer scientist, academic, lecturer, researcher, consultant, and people manager.

This foundation enabled Paul to successfully enter the business of innovation, helping individuals and organizations develop and derive value from their breakthrough ideas. Although it would be untrue to say that his career development was planned, Paul found that by always being open to new ways to make meaningful contributions, he has been able to build on his strengths.

The Third Pillar: Psychological Safety

Psychological safety is all about being able to show up for work as yourself. You do not feel that you need to step into a different "work identity" when you show up in the morning. There is no mask; there is only the authentic you.

You feel accepted for who you are by your management and colleagues. Your experience, your opinions, your diversity, your culture, your strengths, and your imperfections are all respected. People welcome your questions and input. Mistakes that are made in good faith are not just tolerated; they are seen as an opportunity to learn and improve.

In such an environment, people feel that their colleagues and management have their backs. They feel secure and will go above and beyond to contribute to the success of their organization in good times and bad.

The Space Shuttle *Columbia*

On January 16, 2003, the Space Shuttle *Columbia* soared into space. As it climbed, a chunk of foam from the external fuel tank broke free and hit the thermal protection system on the spacecraft's left wing. The shuttle continued its assent into space where the crew began a successful sixteen days of scientific experiments.

Back on Earth, mission control managers believed that the damage from the launch was minimal and would not be a problem for *Columbia*'s return. However, several shuttle engineers who reviewed videos of the launch were concerned that it could trigger a major malfunction. Among them was Rodney Rocha, a chief structural engineer.

Rocha watched the video one day after launch. As he watched, he noticed something that had hit the shuttle during lift-off. Rocha was not sure what he had seen, but he had a feeling that it could be disastrous for the shuttle.

Rocha tried to persuade NASA managers to get telescopic pictures of *Columbia*'s wing before re-entry to better understand the damage, but his requests were ignored. Eight days into the mission, there was a very large mission management team meeting with thirty-five people in the room. The senior people discussed the problem, but Rocha did not speak up about his concerns. Years later, he would say that he did not say anything because he felt that he had to respect seniority.

On February 1, 2003, the Space Shuttle *Columbia* disintegrated upon re-entry, killing the entire crew. This tragedy resulted from the damage that the piece of foam had caused to the Space Shuttle's thermal protection system.

To this day, Rocha regrets not forcing NASA higher-ups to get those pictures and devise a strategy for *Columbia*'s safe return. Here was a smart, experienced engineer who was not willing to speak up about his concerns in a management meeting because he felt psychologically unsafe. Months after the tragic accident the *Columbia* Accident Investigation Board came to the stunning conclusion that the culture in the Space Shuttle Program was as much a cause of the accident as the malfunction on the left wing.

The Fourth Pillar: Reward and Recognition

Timely and meaningful recognition for the work that you do is one of the most important things that can be received. It motivates you for future challenges.

One of the most fundamental rewards that we receive is the salary that we are paid. If we are adding value to the company, we should be compensated. If a person is not being paid an amount commensurate with what they do, that person is more likely to be lured away by a more lucrative offer. However, money and other financial perks are not everything. Meaningful recognition is also important.

There are two aspects of meaningful recognition: recognition related to an accomplishment and recognition for effort, regardless of the outcome. Even the power of a simple "Thank you" should never be underestimated. It does not matter what your position is, who is thanking you, or whom you are thanking. Those two words—which are among the first that we are taught as children—make an impact.

Speaking of children, when they are learning to walk, they spend a lot of time falling. What do their parents do? They cheer them on and praise them for every effort. They recognize the effort that the child is making and encourage them to try again. Why should it be any different for adults in the workplace? Why should recognition for what we do, even when we are not successful, matter any less? It is genuinely disappointing that more people do not exercise this simple yet powerful way to build meaningful connections.

Author's story

When Zsuzsanna received the Global Women Excellence Leadership Award in 2017, it was the most important recognition that she had ever received in her career. She felt proud for several reasons. The nomination had come from her team, it was a worldwide recognition from her employer, and it was an acknowledgement of her achievements.

Yet, the most interesting thing about this award was not the pride that she felt when she received it, but what came after. The recognition that she had received ignited something within her. Zsuzsanna was intensely curious. What had she done to be eligible to receive such a prestigious award? Why her and not one of countless other worthy individuals?

Zsuzsanna wanted to understand the traits of leaders, people who can positively impact others, and what it takes to become one. The recognition of her accomplishments set her on a journey to better understand who she is, why she does what she does, and how she impacts the world. The result has been a series of fascinating discoveries and opportunities, including the writing of this book.

The Fifth Pillar: Promising Future

When you are at work, you spend most of your time focusing on the task at hand. (At least you should be.) It could be a report that you are drafting, a sales pitch that you are making, a meeting that you are attending, or any one of a hundred other things. However, during quiet moments, or even moments when you are not at work, it is likely that your thoughts will, sooner or later, turn to the future.

Do you have a clear idea about where the company is heading, both in terms of its viability, and just as importantly, its mission? Do you have a clear idea where you are heading? Do you see yourself in the company a year from now? Five years from now? Fifteen years from now?

Of course, there are no guarantees that the future will unfold as you imagine it. It is one of the reasons why life is so exciting. Nonetheless, when you feel confident about the future, when you see a clear path forward and how you will travel along that path, it makes for a more rewarding experience at work.

Going global, staying global

Gabriela had about twenty-five years of experience in global companies leading teams when she decided to quit and try something completely different. She took a gap year to explore what she might do. Her father had his own company, and Gabriela had always thought about building something of her own. However, after several months of planning, she realized how much she missed the complex environment of a large company.

Gabriela had always been fascinated by the multitude of moving parts, the international connections, and the high-stake challenges. After several months of reflection, she knew that only this kind of environment could provide her with opportunities to use her strategic thinking capabilities, her deep operational knowledge, and her problem-solving skills. This was how she felt she could make a contribution.

Today, Gabriela works as a Chief Operations Officer at a regional level for a global telecommunications company. When she joined her current company, she felt that she was back in "the zone." Her new company had just acquired another company, so there was a lot of work to do. Gabriela had previously faced similar challenges and successfully led mergers and acquisitions, streamlining other organizations. Because the telecommunications industry was completely new to her, she also had a lot to learn which added an element of positive stress to her job satisfaction.

How solid are your five pillars?

Now that we have set out the five pillars for job satisfaction, it is time to reflect further on your scores in the exercise on page 22. Go back and think for a moment about the scores that you gave. Think about the reasons why you gave a high, low, or medium score for each of those pillars.

EXERCISE: The pillars of your work life

If you are like most people, there are things that you like about your work and things that you dislike. There is a reason why you gave the scores that you did. Let's take a closer look at those reasons.

Using the scrolls below, examine each of the five pillars of your work. For each one, list all the things that you like. These are things that strengthen the pillar. Then, for each pillar, list the things that you do not like. They could be things that are missing or that weaken the pillar.

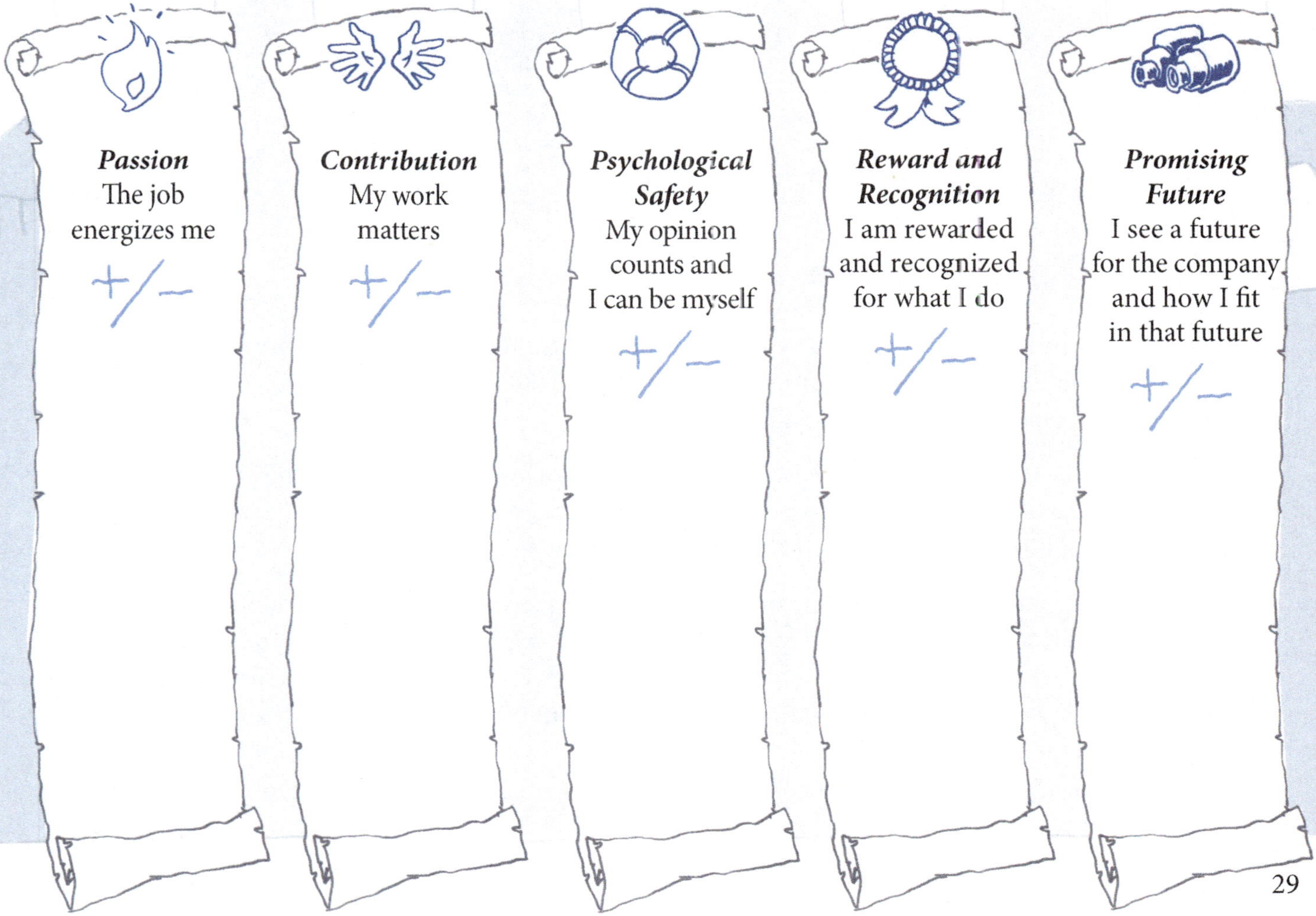

Did the exercise bring any revelations or clarity to your situation? Did you think of positive or negative things that perhaps you had not previously considered? Did you discover anything that would make you reconsider the scores that you gave on page 22?

By reflecting on these five pillars, you will have a better appreciation of how you bring yourself to work and why. If you have had several jobs over the course of your career, you might notice which categories (if any) have had the same score and which (if any) have changed over time.

Perhaps at the beginning of your career, you liked challenging projects and being surrounded by people from whom you could learn, and reward and recognition were less important for you. Maybe you wanted to work for a company that could add credibility to your resume. Over time, the relative importance of these pillars might have shifted. Perhaps working in an environment that matches your personal values became the most important thing for you.

When the job no longer fits

Ioana had been working for approximately five years for a mid-size marketing agency in Bucharest, Romania. She was responsible for the agency's international customers and her role allowed her to travel abroad. She loved her clients, and she loved the work. It was challenging and she felt that her contributions mattered. However, there was a problem.

Every time Ioana thought about her next steps and whether she could see herself in the company for the long term, she was uncertain. One day, she went to see her manager, who was also the owner of the company. During the conversation, it became clear to Ioana that the owner's vision was to keep the company running so that he would make money. There was no plan for the company's growth and little opportunity for her development.

Ioana knew that she had to make a move. For five years, the company had been a great experience for her. She learned a lot and grew professionally. However, given her age and ambitions, Ioana could not see herself in that place anymore, and so she left.

Ioana is excited by the possibilities that lay before her. She feels no need to rush into a new job and is taking her time to reflect on what she wants in her career and whether the companies that she is considering can provide her with what she is looking for.

Your story

In his 2005 commencement speech at Stanford University, Steve Jobs said that he looked in the mirror every morning and asked himself a question: If today were the last day of his life, would he want to do what he was going to do that day? Jobs said that whenever the answer was "No" for too many days in a row, he knew that he needed to change something.

What about you? If you had asked yourself this question this morning, how would you have answered it? How would you have answered it over the course of last week? Last month? Last year? How will you answer it tomorrow?

Think about your current job. What motivated you to choose it? Which of the five pillars (if any) did you consider when making your decision? Did you even have a choice? Did you feel that you had a choice? Or did you take the first opportunity that came along? Maybe you knew some people at the company. Maybe you thought that this is as good as it would get.

EXERCISE: Your story

Thus far, you have read several stories of other people. Now it is time for you to add your own story to these pages.

In the space below, write down how you ended up in your current position. What did you do (or not do) that brought you to your current situation? How much do you enjoy your job and your work environment? What are the key elements that influence your engagement?

Give yourself at least fifteen minutes for this exercise. Use extra paper if necessary.

We do not know what you have written, but we do know that your story is not finished. There is more to come, and you have the opportunity and responsibility to write it.

To do so, we would like you now to take everything that you have read and done thus far in this book and develop your ideas further.

Perfection is a myth, improvement is not

We hope that your current position provides you with the things that are important to you. If it does not, you do not necessarily have to make a radical change. You will, however, have to do some work to see whether you can change your score on page 22 in a positive way.

Please bear in mind that you do not have to score a 10 on each of the five pillars every day of your life. You should not feel frustrated if you occasionally have a low score for any of the pillars. There might be professional or personal reasons that make it difficult for you to concentrate on your work for a while. It happens to everyone. The important thing is to make a commitment to continuous improvement.

Even if you have the intention, courage, and commitment to bring your heart and mind to work, it is not always easy to show up fully. Nevertheless, if you find yourself in a situation where one or more of these pillars have a low score for a prolonged period, it is going to be difficult to feel energized and engaged at work.

It's not just about you

In this chapter, you have started to reflect on your underlying attitudes when you take yourself to work. By working on the exercises, in this and the following chapters, you will develop a clearer idea of what is important to you in your professional life and whether your needs are being met at work.

However, you are not the only player in this game. We must also consider how you relate to your work colleagues. You will spend a lot of time with them, and they will have an impact on your level of satisfaction with your work. That is what the next chapter is all about.

CHAPTER TWO

Being Connected

"Only through our connectedness to others can we really know and enhance the self. And only through working on the self can we begin to enhance our connectedness to others."
– Harriet Lerner

Where are you?

In the previous chapter, you spent time reflecting on your current work environment and how you feel there. In this chapter, we are going to look more deeply at your colleagues and your company. Specifically, we are going to examine how connected you feel to them.

EXERCISE: How connected are you?

Think about your colleagues for a moment. The people with whom you interact every day. Perhaps they work just down the hall from you; perhaps they are in a different time zone and you only communicate with them virtually.

How do you feel about them? How do you relate to them? Do you look forward to connecting with them every day? Do you look forward to working with them?

Now think about the company or organization where you work. What do you know about it? How do you talk about it when speaking with others? Think about some important moments from your work experience and how you felt at the time.

Once you have finished your reflection and connected with the feelings that have arisen, look at the table below. Which section best describes your situation?

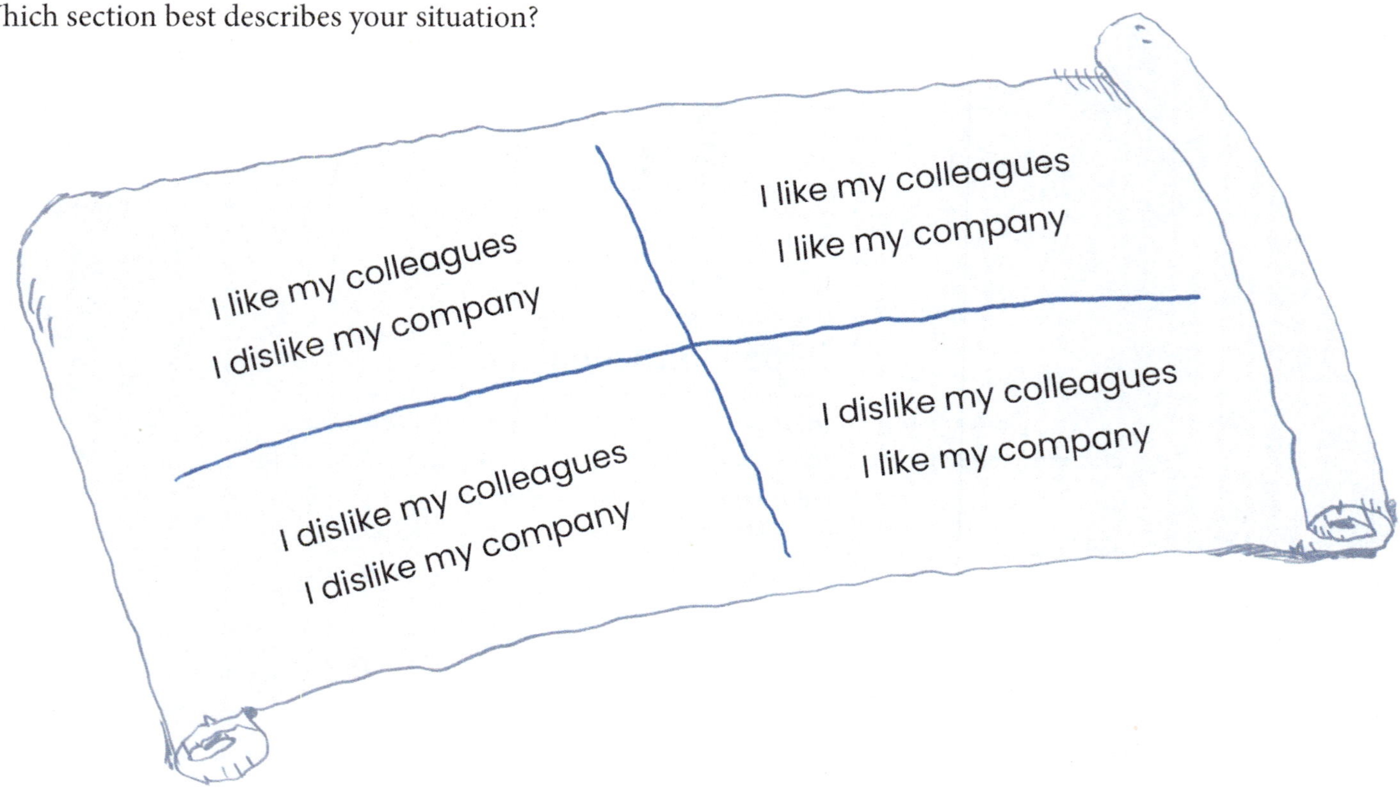

Given the amount of time that you spend at work, you should be in the top right quadrant; you should like your colleagues and your company. If this is the case, congratulations! You are part of the fortunate minority.

When you like the people with whom you work, it adds to your satisfaction. Giving social support to, and receiving it from, others is a key aspect of workplace satisfaction. When you fit in with the organizational culture and your values align with those of the organization, it allows you to feel connected when you are at work.

If you are not in the top right corner of the scroll on the previous page, something needs to change. Perhaps a little, perhaps a lot, because we all need to connect.

The constant gardener

In his book, *Social: Why Our Brains Are Wired to Connect*, Professor Matthew D. Lieberman writes that our need to connect is as fundamental as our need for food and water. People suffer when their social bonds are threatened or weakened or severed. Connection is one of the most important components of a healthy life.

Good connections not only help build a productive and efficient workplace, they also provide an environment that allows employees to flourish by bringing their best selves to work every day. You cannot be disconnected at work, at least not for very long, and hope to have any chance of finding fulfillment.

All the connections that you have at work have one thing in common. They require your personal investment. Building connections is not always easy and it does not happen overnight. It takes effort and constant attention.

In many ways, building connections is like tending a garden. You cannot simply plant the seeds and wait. A garden needs to be constantly nurtured and tended through fertilization, watering, weeding, and harvesting. Building connections cannot be left to the winds of chance. They must be carefully nurtured and have the full buy-in of all concerned.

During the COVID-19 pandemic, a CEO of an IT firm in Spain was interviewed. He was proud to say that his team of one hundred programmers and thirteen support staff were all connected. The interviewers were intrigued to understand how this CEO was measuring that connectedness, so they asked him, "How do you know?"

"Because they all show up on time for our weekly virtual team calls," he said. "I can see their screen times and I know that they are all connected." Sadly, he had completely missed the idea of what it means to be connected in the workplace.

As the discussion continued, it became apparent that this CEO viewed his work as the showpiece of his life; everything else simply fit in around that work. When asked if he personally felt connected in the workplace, he paused with a quizzical look on his face and replied, "Connected to what?"

This CEO's answer is representative of the answer that many people would give. It highlights some of the issues that need to be addressed in the workplace today about being connected.

No man is an island

The 1624 sermon, *For Whom the Bell Tolls*, by the English writer John Donne reads, in part, as follows:

> *No man is an island,*
> *Entire of itself.*
> *Each is a piece of the continent,*
> *A part of the main.*
> . . .
> *Each man's death diminishes me,*
> *Because I am involved in mankind.*

The message is that we are all connected to each other. No one is truly self-sufficient; in order to survive and thrive, everyone must rely on the support of others. The sense of belonging to something greater than yourself is what makes connections with others so important.

When it comes to your work, you have colleagues, clients, bosses, teammates. Even if your job is relatively solitary, there are times when you have to interact with others. How do you connect with those people?

Many people think of connection with their colleagues simply in terms of being able to communicate with them. Communication is certainly important, and we explore this idea further in Chapter 6. Here, however, we are talking about a deeper form of connection, a connection that means you care about people and look out for them.

When you have meaningful connections with the people with whom you work, you feel safe to show up as who you are, and you bring your best self to work. In such a setting it feels natural to work together, share knowledge, overcome difficulties, and celebrate successes.

Connecting people

Nassib Abou-Khalil, the former Chief Legal Officer for Nokia who was responsible for overseeing Nokia's legal affairs and teams worldwide, understands the importance of connection.

When COVID-19 hit, Abou-Khalil, like millions around the world, was forced to work from home. He realized that the quarantine presented challenges, but it also presented opportunities.

Abou-Khalil decided to invest time he would have otherwise spent traveling to engage with his colleagues and get to know them better. He set up one-on-one calls with each person on Nokia's legal and compliance team. There were hundreds of calls in total, but as Abou-Khalil says, it was well worth it:

> "It gave me the opportunity to meet the few individuals that I hadn't met, and to get to know each person at an individual level. I felt truly blessed because the people on the team gave me the time, opened their hearts, and shared generously. And I felt that after each call, I had managed to build a very strong bond with each individual with whom I had spoken. And honestly, I cannot describe how grateful and happy I felt.
>
> "Truly, it gave me first-hand, real tangible insight into how people were living this pandemic and how people felt. I felt connected, I felt that I understood the situations that some people were going through, the difficulties that they were facing. And I felt that I learned enough about them to be able to share key messages and to share insights, and to bring the entire team together as a community that is spread around the globe. And that was truly remarkable."

Abou-Khalil's initiative goes to the heart of what it means to make a conscious effort to connect with people at the workplace.

More than a feeling

It is important to be connected with others at work, but what exactly does that mean? We put this question to several employees, managers, and entrepreneurs. The responses varied, but one of the simplest was: "It's a feeling and you just know it."

True, but there is more to it than that.

Being connected at work with your colleagues is like being a member of a high-performance sports team. Players train together, travel together, share information with each other, and play together, all for the common goal of winning.

Players know that they can only win as a team; that is what creates a deeper connection between and among them. What they can achieve together is greater than what any individual can achieve alone.

Each person on the team has a role, each person understands that role, and each person knows that they must perform that role to the best of their ability.

When a team wins, the coaches and players celebrate together. When a team loses, they openly discuss what they could have done differently. It is only when they have each other's back that they feel safe to acknowledge mistakes, share ideas to improve, and learn together.

It is no different in the workplace.

Print run panic

In 2012, a small publishing company in the United Kingdom was tasked with producing 100,000 business directories. To get the job done, the publishing company had secured a contract with one of the UK's top printers.

To guarantee that they would not miss the print run, the printer gave the publishing company a deadline for the delivery of all the files. Three days before the deadline, the publishing company had completed the work and sent the files to the printer. It then gave its employees a few days off for some well-deserved rest after a long campaign.

However, twenty-four hours before the deadline, the publishing company received a distressing email from the printer. Some of the files were in the wrong format and others were corrupted. Disaster loomed.

The Marketing Director of the publishing company called the printer and promised that the problem would be resolved before the deadline. The Marketing Director then called the members of his team on their day off and explained the situation. Every member came in and worked around the clock to reformat the files, double check them and ensure that they met the deadline.

What is special about this story is that when the Marketing Director explained the situation to his colleagues, no one complained. Everyone dropped what they had been doing and came to the office. They ordered pizzas and drinks, played inspirational music, and worked through the night to get the job done. It is a great example of what happens when people feel connected and committed to their colleagues.

Connected teams adhere to the wisdom of the American President Harry Truman who said, "It is amazing what you can accomplish when you do not care who gets the credit." In such an environment, it feels natural to work together, share knowledge, celebrate success, and overcome difficulties.

EXERCISE: Connecting with colleagues

Can you think of a time when you had a great connection at work with your colleagues? What were you working on? What skills were you using? How did you relate to your colleagues? What were the shared values and objectives?

As you reflect, complete the following sentence:

Things worked well because …

Now think about a time when you and your colleagues did not work together as well as you could have. Was there a difference in values? Was there a lack of clarity? How did you communicate with each other? What was the outcome?

As you reflect, complete the following sentence:

Things did not work well because …

Connections can be broken

Let's imagine a hypothetical situation that is representative of something that happens often in the business world.

Joe is part of the product management team at his company. Joe's team is responsible for bringing new products to market. Before the company's senior executives will invest a single dollar in a new product, Joe and his team must convince them to support the idea.

On a Friday morning, Joe receives an email from one of the senior executives. She tells Joe that the executive team is having second thoughts about the new product that Joe has been working on for the past several months. They are inclined to cancel it but are willing to give Joe a chance to defend his idea and present the business rationale the following Wednesday.

Joe, who has other pressing deadlines, sends a brief email to Matt, his colleague in the marketing department, and asks him to update the PowerPoint slides on the product for a presentation on Wednesday.

Friday passes, Monday morning passes, but still no update from Matt.

Joe has always prided himself on being a good colleague who collaborates well with others. However, there is so much at stake with this product, that he cannot wait any longer for an update. Joe calls Matt, and in exasperation, asks, "What's happening with the deck?! Why isn't it ready?! Where is it?"

Matt is confused. Normally, he and Joe work well together and he cannot understand why Joe is so upset. Matt was just finishing the updates to the presentation and now, here is Joe, speaking to him as though he were a junior employee. Matt is angry but keeps his thoughts to himself as he sends the updated slides to Joe.

What just happened? Perhaps Joe could have given Matt clearer instructions about the urgency of the matter and a specific time by which he needed an updated presentation. Perhaps Joe could have spoken to Matt at the beginning instead of sending him an email. Perhaps Matt could have asked for clarification from Joe about the matter. What we do know is that although there was an external dialogue between Joe and Matt (written and spoken), each is playing an internal dialogue in his mind.

Joe cannot understand why Matt, a senior product marketing lead, is taking this situation so lightly. Joe is stressed and afraid, not only for the product in which he has invested so much time, but also for his position. Meanwhile Matt feels betrayed by Joe. It seems that Joe no longer trusts him and now is treating him like a junior employee.

In this situation, the connection between Joe and Matt has become frayed, but it did not have to reach this state. The two men could have had a different conversation, one in which they not only heard the words spoken by the other, but also listened to what the other truly needed. If both men had openly shared their needs and concerns, the relationship would not have been harmed, and indeed, could have been strengthened.

EXERCISE: Meaningful connections

Reflect on the situation above between Joe and Matt and think of meaningful connections at your workplace. Capture your insights using the below table:

What does it mean being connected to my colleagues at work?	
What do I need from them to feel connected to them?	
What do they need from me to create meaningful connections between us?	
What is present when I feel connected?	
What is missing when I don't feel connected?	

Connections can be strengthened

Have you experienced a situation similar to that of Joe and Matt in the example above? A situation where you felt that your colleagues were not listening to your needs? Or perhaps you realized after the fact that you had not listened to the needs of your colleagues? How did you feel?

What can you do to improve your relationship with your colleagues and learn to listen to the unspoken conversations that might be taking place? Below are three ideas for you to consider.

Get to know me

One simple thing that you can do that will pay dividends in your work relationships is to get to know your colleagues better. Spend some time finding out about the things that they like and dislike. In this same spirit, if you share information about yourself, your colleagues will come to know you better.

No matter how busy your job is, you almost certainly can find a few moments every day—at lunch or over coffee—to speak with your colleagues and learn more about them, their families, their hobbies, their likes, their dislikes, their successes, their struggles. These types of meaningful conversations can have a bigger impact in the long run than the typical functional and transactional conversations that usually take place at work.

We are not suggesting that every aspect of your life should be open to your colleagues. We all have things that we want to remain private. The point is that sharing something about yourself with your colleagues, when appropriate, might just be the thing that is needed to strengthen the bonds between you.

Foundational feedback

Another thing that you can do is encourage your colleagues to provide you with constructive feedback. It is a great opportunity for your personal development, and it also shows humility and respect on your part. When you encourage others to provide feedback, they will likely be more open to receiving feedback from you.

When feedback is shared in a spirit of wanting to help each other, the foundations of work relationships are solidified. Feedback is a great way to discover your blind spots, i.e., things that you do not know about yourself. Such blind spots are not only about things for you to improve; they can also be about your strengths. You may have skills and talents that you do not often think about, but which mean a lot to others.

When you work in an environment where sharing feedback about each other is part of your culture, you form deeper connections and have a higher appreciation of each other. We will speak more about feedback in different contexts throughout the book.

The magical mystery tour

The most mysterious, and in many ways the most magical, connections happen when you go through new experiences together as a team. When you spend time together at an offsite event, who knows what hidden gems might be discovered?

Talents, insights, tastes, feelings, capabilities, strengths, weaknesses, all of which were previously unknown, reveal themselves in different situations when your reactions or skills are put to the test. The revelations spawned by these new experiences can allow people to see their colleagues in a whole new light, creating a unique sense of connectedness.

Sharing new experiences as a team can lead to some of the most meaningful and unexpected connections. Whether it's an escape room, cooking class, karaoke night or other offsite event, these activities can reveal hidden talents and strengths in your team members.

When your team is put to the test in new situations, it can also give you a fresh perspective on your colleagues, fostering a unique sense of camaraderie. When planning team-building activities, keep in mind the personalities and preferences of your team members. Not every team is the same, so what may be an exciting adventure for one team, might not be suitable for another. Choose an activity that pushes everyone out of their comfort zones, but is still fun and enjoyable for all.

EXERCISE: Strengthening connections

Take some time to reflect on the ideas above and how you could use them to strengthen the connections between you and your colleagues. Perhaps you have already tried one or more of them. If so, great! Reflect on what you learned about or from, your team members and how it felt to share something about yourself. What happened to you as a team when you shared new experiences together? How did it impact your relationship?

Now, regardless of whether you have done any of these things in the past, think of three things that you can do in the future to strengthen your connections with your colleagues.

Sawubona: A deep level of connection

One of the official languages of South Africa is Zulu (*isiZulu* in Zulu), which is spoken by about ten million people. There is a word in Zulu—*Sawubona*—that means, "I see you." Not in the sense of, "I see you standing before me, and I see that you are wearing blue jeans and sweater, and I see that your hair is done up today, and I see that you are wearing your glasses instead of contact lenses." *Sawubona* is more than that.

At its heart, *Sawubona* means, "I see you as a person who has a history and a culture and a family. I see you as a person with hopes and fears, with wants and needs, with dreams and ambitions. I see you and I value the time that we have together." It is an invitation to participate in each other's lives. It requires genuine concern and caring for the other person.

Being connected to your colleagues often depends on the nature of the projects in which you are involved. Never forget, however, that the people with whom you work are individuals with lives that are as rich and complex as yours. They have hopes and dreams and fears and insecurities too. They are people who want to be seen, understood, and maybe even helped.

As you work on building connections at work, think about the people with whom you are trying to connect. What insights can you share with them? How can you make their lives a little bit easier? How can you help them work through a problem? How can you have a conversation with them, and possibly about them, at least from time to time?

Whenever you sit down with your colleagues, in a meeting or at lunch or when working on a project, pause for a moment at the outset and think, "*Sawubona*. I see you."

Follow the leader

According to Gallup's 2015 *State of the American Manager* Report, only 35% of managers in the United States are engaged in their jobs. Moreover, the report states that 50% of employees have, at some point in their career, quit their job just to get away from their manager. That's right, these employees have quit, not because of the work or the salary, but because of poor management. Think about that for a moment!

Statistics like these send a strong message. Even if you have stimulating work, a great relationship with your colleagues, and great pay and benefits, it can all be undone by a bad manager. If your manager does not create an engaging environment, there is a good chance that you will start to look for opportunities elsewhere.

Rasmus Hougaard is the founder and managing partner of Potential Project. Hougaard and his organization completed two years of research in collaboration with the *Harvard Business Review*. They surveyed more than 35,000 business leaders from more than 120 countries and 900 companies. They interviewed more than 200 CEOs and C-suite leaders of global companies.

One of the key takeaways from this research was that leaders need to be better at creating a culture that focuses on people. What does this mean in practice? What are the leadership characteristics of great managers who can build and maintain engaging environments for their people?

A starting point to answer these questions is to understand the characteristics of bad leadership and then to look for the opposite.

The Predictive Index 2018 People Management Study asked 5,103 employees to identify bad leadership qualities. Here are the top ten that they identified:

If these are bad leadership qualities, what are the good ones?

In a 2014 article in *The Harvard Business Review* entitled "The Skills Leaders Need at Every Level," leadership development consultants Jack Zenger and Joseph Folkman discussed the results of a study that they conducted on the skills that leaders need to succeed. They asked more than 300,000 business leaders to rank the top ten competencies from a list of sixteen key leadership skills. The results were as follows:

EXERCISE: What leadership means to you

From the above-listed good and bad leadership qualities, which ones are the most important for you? In your opinion, which good qualities must a manager absolutely have? Which bad qualities would move you to leave or at least seek a different job in the same organization?

Now, think about your current manager. What role does that person play in your life? What does he or she do to make you feel connected? What, if anything, is missing? If you do not currently have a manager, which good qualities would be essential, and which bad qualities would be dealbreakers, for a potential manager in the future?

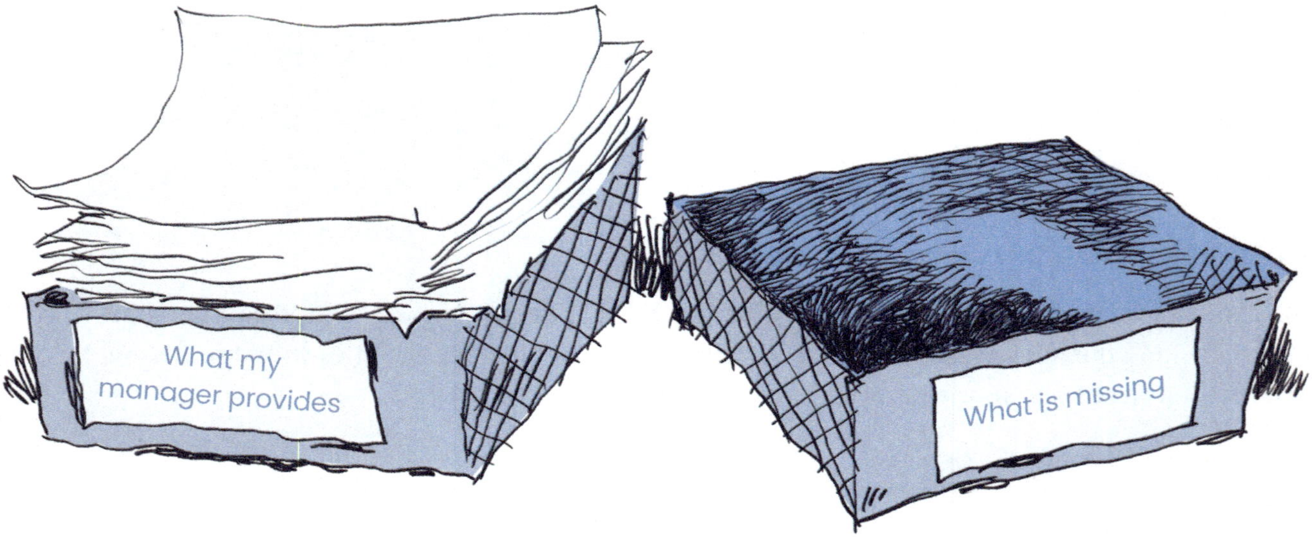

The corporate connection

It is undeniably a good feeling to be in a stimulating environment where you have great connections with your colleagues and your manager. But what about the company or organization? What does it mean to be connected with your company?

Being connected to your company is more than just doing the work and more than just social engagement. It is about whether you share the values, vision, and mission of the company and whether you have a sense that you belong there.

St. Paul's Cathedral

Christopher Wren was a seventeenth-century English architect and one of the most highly acclaimed architects in history. He designed London's famous St. Paul's Cathedral which overlooks the River Thames. There is a story that one day Wren went to the work site in a disguise so that the workers would not recognize him. He walked around and talked to some of the men.

"What are you doing?" Wren asked one of the workmen who was bent over his work.

The man, who was a bit surprised by the question, replied, "I'm cutting a piece of stone for this wall."

As Wren carried on walking around the worksite, he asked the same question to another man who was sawing some wood. The man replied, "I'm earning six shillings a day as a carpenter."

Continuing his walk around the worksite, Wren posed the same question to a third man who was building a scaffold. The man thought for a moment and said, "I'm helping to build a cathedral. This cathedral will be here for our children, our children's children and for generations to come."

All three men had clearly defined tasks that motivated them to carry out their work; however, only the third man was fully aligned with the vision of building the cathedral. He could see beyond the labor that he did or the wage that he earned. He was part of an endeavor to create a work of art, a great cathedral. Unlike the first two workers, the third man was fully aligned to the mission and vision that Christopher Wren had inspired. When someone is fully engaged like this, they feel a strong sense of belonging.

If someone asked you what you do, how would you respond? Would you be like the third man in the story or like one of the other workers?

The Fantastic Four

There are many aspects that define your connection with the company where you work. It is not just about your colleagues and managers. What do you like about your company or organization? When this question was asked on an online community platform some key elements emerged from the hundreds of responses.

When people like a company, they:

Feel that their personal **values** align with the company's culture.

See how their personal **aspirations** can be linked to the vision and mission of their organization.

Feel that they are **trusted** and that they can trust others.

Can be **themselves** when coming to work.

It comes down to alignment. Alignment between who you are and what your company is.

It's a process

As circumstances and priorities change, it takes a continuous process of dialogue and adaptation to be connected to your company and your colleagues. Nevertheless, it is worth the effort. Consider these facts:

- Positive connections in the workplace reduce stress hormones and increase the neurotransmitters responsible for attention, feelings of pleasure, and trust.
- Some of your best friends, business partners or even life partners can be found in the workplace.
- When you feel connected, you are more likely to offer new ideas to new projects and thus become even more valuable in the workplace.
- Time flies when you are in a fun environment.

When you work at a company, you demonstrate daily how you benefit the company and its stakeholders. But you also have a responsibility to yourself. You should feel connected to the company for which you work and the people with whom you work. Otherwise, it is going to be hard to remain motivated for very long.

And motivation is precisely what we are going to discuss in the next chapter.

CHAPTER THREE

Motivation and Me

"True success is attained only through the satisfaction of knowing you did everything within the limits of your ability to become the very best that you are capable of being."
– John Wooden

What motivates you?

What motivates someone to wake up every day at 4:00 a.m. for four years to train for a sporting competition that will only last a few minutes or even a few seconds? Why would someone dedicate their lives to flying to the edge of space just to come back down almost immediately afterwards?

Why have you continued to read this book? You have made it to Chapter 3. What has kept you going? What will keep you going to the end?

More generally, which of your needs must be met to keep you motivated? A need in this sense is something that is necessary for you to be able to live a healthy and fulfilling life. It might be personal, social, cultural, physical, professional. A need is something that evokes an emotional response, one that is positive when the need is met, and negative when it is not.

Motivation is what helps you when you want to achieve a goal, which in turn will meet a specific need. Motivation moves you to act and sustains you when the going gets tough. It is a complex mix of biological, emotional, social, and cognitive factors which when analyzed through the lens of your personal values, enables you to make conscious choices about how you meet your own needs by achieving selected goals.

Today, there are countless books about our relationship with motivation, and more specifically, motivation in relation to the work that we do. Centuries ago, most people would have been happy with a job that satisfied the need to buy enough food for their families and to keep a roof over their heads. Having a job was good enough.

Of course, there is more to life than just having a job. No matter what you do, as we have already seen, you should be motivated to bring your best self to your work every day.

In this chapter, you will continue to explore how you relate to work, but this time we invite you to go deeper. We want you to take a good look at yourself so that you better understand your personal values and how they relate to your motivations. You will find out how to recognize what motivates you. You will look at different types of motivation so that you can recognize the things that keep you energetic and focused, as opposed to the things that drain your energy.

Can we pick your brain?

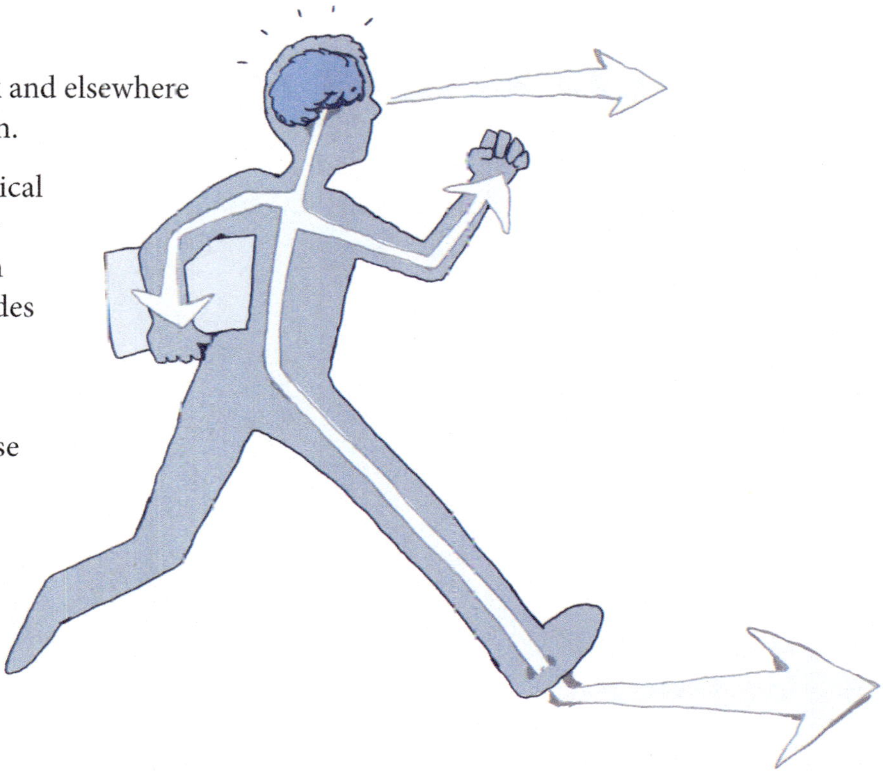

The importance of being motivated at work and elsewhere is rooted in science. It all begins in the brain.

In the brain, neurotransmitters spark chemical messages to keep us alert and focused, they allow nerve cells to communicate with each other across synapses. The brain then decodes these messages.

When it comes to happiness and success, four hormones play an important role. These neurotransmitters are dopamine, oxytocin, serotonin, and endorphin (collectively referred to as "DOSE"). They are also known as "success hormones," because apart from a happy mood, they give you optimism, energy, and a higher focus. They elevate your drive and confidence at work.

Of the four, dopamine is your achievement hormone. It is the motivation molecule that drives you to seek rewards when achieving goals and enables you to make the effort required to be successful. Dopamine triggers feedback for predicting rewards. Your brain recognizes that something good is about to happen and the dopamine kicks in.

This form of motivation manifests itself by our desire to maximize pleasure or minimize pain. Interestingly, dopamine performs its function before we obtain rewards. In other words, dopamine encourages us to act, either to achieve something good or to avoid something bad.

Let's look more closely at motivation.

Types of Motivation

Take a few moments to reflect on your relationship with motivation. When do you feel most motivated? When do you lack motivation? Everyone is different and your motivation can vary in different situations. Put the book down now and think about what motivates you to take action.

Now that you have finished your reflection, read through the following types of motivation that can influence behavior. Read the descriptions for each and think about whether, and how, they relate to your own motivation.

Meaning

Are you motivated by the desire to have meaning in your life? Viktor Frankl was a renowned psychologist who survived the horrors of the Auschwitz concentration camp. He wrote the classic, *Man's Search for Meaning*, in which he shared his thoughts about the reasons why those who survived the camps did so. He concluded that it was because they had some mission, some purpose, which they had to fulfill. According to Frankl, the search for meaning is the primary, intrinsic motivation of human beings.

Improvement and accomplishment

Look around your office at work or at home. Do you have medals, certificates, and memorabilia of your achievements on show? If so, this would indicate that you are motivated by the desire for improvement and accomplishments. Having a sense of accomplishment and a feeling of pride about your achievements helps you feel like you are progressing.

This form of motivation is not just about the accumulation of accolades. A sense of achievement can also come from the desire to complete an item on your to-do list or complete a long-term project for a client. The motivational high that you experience from accomplishing a task can be important. According to the Happiness Research Institute in Denmark, the desire to reach goals is the fourth most important influencer in employee engagement.

Ownership

Think of your most prized possession. Is it your house, your car, your wedding ring or perhaps an object which has a special sentimental value? Maybe you are still working towards purchasing something upon which you place great value. What does that possession mean to you? What would you do to acquire or keep it? If you are motivated by the desire for ownership, you have an emotional connection with the possession.

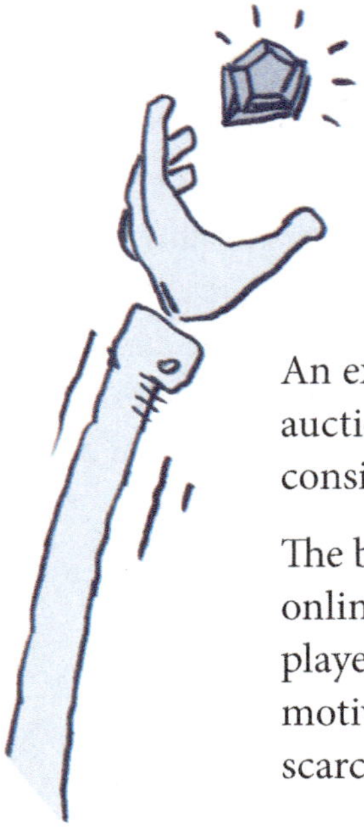

Scarcity and Exclusivity

In his work on the power of persuasion, Dr. Robert Cialdini cites scarcity as one of the key principles of persuasion. Are you motivated by "once in a lifetime" opportunities? Or is your motivation based on FOMO (the fear of missing out)?

An extreme example of how people are motivated by scarcity and exclusivity is the famous auction for Paul Newman's legendary 1968 Rolex Cosmograph Daytona. Many aficionados consider this watch to be one of the most iconic of the twentieth century.

The bidding began at USD $1 million. Driven by an overwhelming desire for ownership, an online bidder went straight in with a bid for USD $10 million, instantly wiping out the small players. For the next thirteen minutes, the auction swung to-and-fro between two highly motivated buyers and eventually, the watch sold for USD $15.5 million. If the desire to have scarce and exclusive things is one of your main motivations, you are in elite company.

Social Pressure

Social pressure can motivate you to do things because you want to do what everybody else is doing (or what you think that others expect you to do). Too often, of course, social pressure is a negative influence. The pressure that you feel from peers and society can move you to do things that deep down, you do not want to do. An illustration of how this works is the famous Abilene Paradox, a concept introduced by Jerry Harvey in the journal *Organizational Dynamics* in 1974.

According to an anecdote recounted by Harvey, a family (husband, wife, and the wife's parents) were sitting on the porch one hot summer afternoon in Texas enjoying some lemonade and a game of dominoes. At one point, the wife's father proposed that they all go to Abilene for dinner. To do so, they would have to go on a long car ride. One by one, the members of the family agreed with the suggestion. So, they all drove for an hour in the hot, dusty weather to the restaurant.

After a less-than-successful dinner and a long, hot drive back home, everyone said that it had not been an enjoyable experience. Furthermore, one by one, they each admitted that they had not really wanted to go in the first place. Even the father said that he had only suggested it because he thought that everyone was bored. Nobody had spoken up because each person thought that everyone else wanted to go.

It is an example of groupthink where peer pressure encourages people to go along with ideas with which they do not agree. Can you think of examples when you have been motivated by social pressure?

Creativity and Feedback

Are you more creative when you feel motivated, or are you more motivated when you are being creative? Research shows that creative people are more likely to experience higher levels of intrinsic motivation. However, when they do not have the required amounts of intrinsic motivation, their creativity is diminished.

Is the satisfaction that you get from your creativity important to you? How does your desire for, or aversion to, feedback affect creativity? Is feedback an important part of your motivation to express your creativity?

Loss Avoidance

Loss avoidance is the tendency to prefer the security of avoiding a loss over the potential for a gain. It is why some people do not invest in risky stocks or engage in physical sports or try a new, unfamiliar job. Do you take steps to avoid losing something? For example, do you feel the desire to take out extra holiday insurance just in case something goes wrong?

Of course, it is important to take reasonable precautions; by all means, wear your seatbelt and read the instructions. However, if you routinely avoid any type of risk to preserve what you have, it can have negative consequences over time and severely limit your opportunities.

Unpredictability

Do you enjoy the buzz and excitement that comes with not knowing the outcome of a situation? Are you motivated when you venture into the unknown? For example, do you like traveling to new countries or going to the casino for some fun on the slot machines? Are you willing to eat at an exotic restaurant that serves cuisine that you have never tried before?

This sense of unpredictability can be a strong motivator. It opens up new experiences and can stretch you to use your skills in unexpected situations.

Intrinsic and extrinsic motivation

Psychologists have proposed different ways to think about motivation. They include looking at whether your motivation arises from personal internal factors (intrinsic motivation) or external factors (extrinsic motivation).

Understanding your motivation regarding your work is important, especially when it comes to making decisions (a topic that we examine in Chapter 7). When your overriding motivations are extrinsic, you will be motivated to behave or engage in an activity, because of your need to earn a reward or avoid punishment. You engage in behavior not because you enjoy it or find it satisfying, but because you expect to get something in return or avoid something unpleasant.

When you engage in an activity based on intrinsic motivation, you do it because you find it satisfying or fulfilling. You perform the activity for its own sake rather than the desire for some external reward. Doing the activity is its own reward.

Two people can do the same activity for different reasons. One person might be extrinsically motivated and the other intrinsically motivated. Some examples are listed in the table below.

Intrinsic Motivation	**Extrinsic Motivation**
Participating in a sport because you find the activity enjoyable	Participating in a sport to win awards
Studying because you enjoy learning	Studying to receive accolades from others
Entering a competition for the challenge	Entering a competition to win a medal
Taking a job because the values of the company align with yours	Taking a job because of the prestigious name of the company
Accepting a promotion because of the challenge it offers to learn and grow	Accepting a promotion because of the company car and a corner office

A balancing act

The interplay between extrinsic and intrinsic motivation can be complex. Extrinsic motivation is beneficial in some cases. Working towards a reward can be helpful when you need to complete a task you might normally find unpleasant. For example, you might not like doing your taxes every year, who does? But the sooner you do them, the sooner you will get that refund (or avoid a penalty for filing late).

However, relying solely on extrinsic motivation to do a task can lose its effectiveness over time, particularly if the reward is taken away or the rules for obtaining the reward are changed. Take, for example, a company that has a "Top Achievers" award that is given to salespeople who meet a yearly sales target. If this extrinsic motivation is suddenly taken away, but the salesperson is still expected to meet the sales target to receive a full salary, it would be demotivating for many people.

Intrinsic motivation is a more effective and more sustainable method for achieving goals and completing tasks. You are self-driven and the achievement itself is what makes you feel fulfilled.

The ideal situation is to have harmony and balance between your intrinsic and extrinsic motivation. For example, your reward for helping a client achieve record sales might be both a significant bonus (extrinsic) and the satisfaction that comes from knowing that you applied your skills to the best of your ability to help other people be successful (intrinsic).

A conversation with God

Money and time, time and money. Two significant motivators.

Time after time

Many people today feel as though they do not have enough time to fulfill all their responsibilities, whether those responsibilities are job-related (such as completing work assignments) or personal (such as organizing things at home or dealing with family emergencies). Do you ever have days (weeks, months) when you feel that life is a constant race against the clock? Having more time is an increasingly important motivator for many people.

People want some level of control over their lives, and they want to feel like they are in control. As the dynamic (many would say hectic) pace of corporate life only shows signs of accelerating, more and more employees are looking for alternatives that give them more time.

The COVID-19 pandemic's enforced slowdown (or shutdown) of many offices created stresses, financial and otherwise, for many people. But it also gave them time; in some cases, more time than they had had in years. Many people have realized the value of this time and are not willing to give it up. And, when companies provide flexibility to their employees to manage their own time, they feel more motivated and connected.

Time affluence is an important intrinsic motivation. An example of time affluence can be seen in companies that provide flexibility to their employees to manage their own time. Flexible working hours is an attractive extrinsic motivation for many people.

It often turns out that time, not money, is a better indicator of happiness and a strong motivation for many. But money still counts.

Show me the money

If you could pay yourself as much money as you wanted, how much would it be? Once you have a number, imagine that you are being paid that amount right now. Will that amount of money keep you motivated?

Intuitively, one might think that higher pay would produce better results and more motivation. However, studies indicate that the link between compensation, motivation, and performance is more complex. In fact, research suggests that even if people could choose how much they earned, they would probably not perform any better or enjoy their job more.

There is ample evidence to suggest that money is not necessarily the best way to motivate desirable behavior. It might, in fact, be one of the worst. In his book *Drive: The Surprising Truth About What Motivates Us*, Daniel Pink found that offering contingent rewards, including money, for complex, creative tasks did little to improve performance, and sometimes even reduced it. Pink found that intrinsic motivators such as autonomy, mastery, and purpose are much more effective.

Money is often used as a default motivator because it is measurable and tangible. Indeed, studies show that up to a certain point, money is a positive motivator. For example, an unemployed person who manages to get a job earning USD $60,000 a year will be happier and more motivated than he was previously. He can put a roof over his family's head, food on the table, and even be able to afford a modest vacation.

The dilemma comes when money is the main—and perhaps only—motivation. Beyond a certain point, money ceases to be a motivator. Paying someone more does not necessarily mean they will perform better in their job, or even stay in the same company.

Motivation in the workplace

Take a moment to reflect on the job that you are doing today. What are the factors driving your fulfillment and happiness? Are you motivated by your salary? Are your position and title important to you? Are you motivated by the opportunity to make a difference in the lives of your customers? Do the people you work with motivate you? Is having the autonomy to do your work at your own pace important for you?

It is important to be aware of your intrinsic motivation in your workplace. It is also important that you have a clear understanding of the extrinsic motivation that is provided by the work that you do, the workplace environment, and company that you work for.

EXERCISE: Your motivators at work

In the table on the next page, list your top five motivators in your work. Then write down whether they are intrinsic, extrinsic, or perhaps both.

Motivator	Intrinsic	Extrinsic

A (parking) lot of motivation

There is a beautiful National Park just north of Barcelona which boasts some of the most incredible hiking routes in Spain. Before embarking on any of the routes, you must leave your car in a municipal parking lot and start your hike from there.

The parking lot attendant's name is Montse. For more than ten years, her role has been to greet drivers on arrival, direct them to the park and give them a ticket. Montse does this job Monday to Saturday, 9:00 a.m. to 6:00 p.m., rain or shine. And every single day, she always has a big smile on her face and a kind word to say to each visitor.

One day, a regular hiker asked Montse why she was so cheerful all the time. Her answer was revealing. "I work in nature with wonderful views of the mountains. This feeds my need to be connected with nature. Why shouldn't I be happy and share that happiness with others?"

Montse's answer brings us to the "sweet spot" of motivation. To be motivated in your job, your job has to meet your needs. Montse has a need to be connected with nature; her happiness at being outdoors and her desire to share this experience with others provides her with intrinsic motivation.

A change in the wind

Over time, the things that motivate you, be they intrinsic or extrinsic, can change. Consequently, a work-life situation that was once ideal might no longer be the right place for you. There is a danger whenever there is a mismatch between your needs and the motivation to meet those needs from the work that you do.

You may have discovered that being able to use your creativity is one of your needs and an important source of intrinsic motivation. However, suppose that in your job, there is little room for creative expression. Initially, the tension that exists between your need to be creative and your work environment might not be noticeable. Over time, however, your inability to put your creativity to use can lead to a lack of productivity and low morale. In an extreme case, it can affect your mental health.

Becoming the (semi)conductor of his own life

Samir spent ten years working as a customer service agent for a semiconductor company. He felt disengaged from the job, the product, and the company. When asked why he had stayed with the job for so long, Samir said that it paid well and came with a decent pension package.

Samir found himself in a toxic trap: happy with the money, not happy at work. Because he was good at his job (and at pretending that he loved it), one day Samir was offered a promotion opportunity that was the envy of his colleagues. Instead, all Samir saw was the threat of going deeper into a hole that was not of his choosing.

While fretting about what to do, Samir had a revelation. He realized that the common denominator in his toxic situations was himself. When the work was piling up, he was there. When the meetings dragged on, he was there. When the clients were too demanding, he was there. Samir understood that in every case, the one thing over which he had control was his attitude toward what was happening.

Samir realized that although he was performing at a high level in the company, his motivation had left him a long time ago. He was simply going through the motions of the job, yet still able to keep up the façade. Being offered the promotion forced him to face the reality that he was unhappy, and things had to change. Faced with this insight, Samir realized that he had five choices:

1. Stay in his current job and be unhappy
2. Rekindle his motivation for the current job
3. Take the promotion but continue hating the job
4. Take the promotion and love the job
5. Leave the company and look for something else

By thinking deeply about his personal situation as well as key aspects of his work life, Samir was able to connect with what was important to him and create a clear list of his intrinsic motivators. This gave him the confidence to not only co-create his new role with management, but also to negotiate a salary and incentive package (the extrinsic motivators) that included a clear, sustainable path for his personal development, ensuring that he would bring his best self to work every day.

Today, Samir is one of the key members of the company and is responsible for running a high-achieving team as well as managing a substantial budget. He says that there are even more demands placed on his time, but he has learned how to manage that time as well as the time of others. Samir is now strongly connected with his personal values and what motivates him. He feels fulfilled in his work life.

When motivation fails

Motivation is important, but motivation is also unreliable. An external event might shatter your motivation. On the other hand, you might lose interest in your work for no apparent reason.

In your pursuit of a balanced and rewarding work life, not everything will be fun and enjoyable all the time. There will inevitably be some decisions and events that affect your level of motivation. The discipline to focus on understanding your needs and how you are being motivated to meet those needs is crucial in these situations.

Author's story

Tony is a practitioner of tai chi in Barcelona. His teacher, Master Pan Zenchai, teaches a small group of dedicated students who come from different parts of the city to learn from his forty-five years of experience. He chooses his students carefully, not based on their level of motivation, but on their level of discipline.

During the first few weeks, Pan Zenchai asks his students to learn a series of repetitive breathing movements which can easily seem boring and inconsequential. He keeps a watchful eye on the students as they perform these exercises. During this time, he can accurately predict those who will last past the first six months and those who will drop out as a result of decreasing motivation.

What Pan Zenchai does not tell his students—and what Tony came to discover—is that after the discipline of learning the basics of breathing and focused movement in tai chi, there comes a huge surge of internal satisfaction as one begins to experience the connection between breathing and a sense of well-being. You can literally control your mood with your breathing. For committed practitioners of tai chi, this ancient martial art is an integral part of their daily rituals.

Being aware of things that can impact your motivation is also important. With this awareness, you can develop the discipline to manage situations when they arise. The reasons why people lose motivation are many, but they include:

- Boredom
- Lack of confidence in one's abilities
- Unambitious objectives
- Unrealistic expectations
- Lack of preparation
- Personal loss
- Change of manager or teammates
- Loss of personal identity
- Feeling unappreciated

With regard to your work, can you think of examples when your motivation declined? Perhaps there were times when your role was not as challenging as you had hoped it would be. Maybe the boss who hired you left and was replaced by a new boss with whom you felt little connection. Perhaps you were promoted to a position and were afraid that it would shine a light on your shortcomings.

In a rare lunch retreat with his students, Pan Zenchai shared an important insight. It takes seven years to master the basics of the movement of tai chi, another seven years to master the art of integrating the movements with your breathing, and yet another seven years during which students begin the deeper internal journey into the true benefits of the art. It is only after twenty-one years of tai chi practice that someone is truly ready to learn the art of tai chi.

This wisdom was not lost on the group. The students understood that the journey would take them through thrilling highs and humbling lows of self-discovery. Along the way, they would build habits and rituals that would allow them to find inner strength, peace, and importantly, the motivation to pass through anything that life might throw at them.

Your company's responsibility

Different people are motivated by different things. Do you know people who fit any of the following descriptions?

- The person who is motivated by competition. If there is an award for best salesperson at the end of the year, these people are determined to get it. If someone is on the treadmill next to them in the gym, they are determined to run faster and longer.

- The person who is motivated by recognition. If they do a good job, they expect to be acknowledged for their efforts, ideally in public.

- The person who is motivated by community. They value their relationships at work and their connections to others. They want to be part of a community in which people trust and support each other.

- The person who is motivated by autonomy. These people do not like being micromanaged; they want to be able to make their own decisions on matters of consequence.

We could extend this list a long way. The point is that motivation comes in all shapes and sizes and is something about which companies need to be aware.

The issue of who is responsible for motivation in the workplace is one that has been studied, trialed, and debated over many years. Most companies believe that they have a responsibility in this regard. Various approaches have been taken to implement these motivational initiatives. You might be familiar with examples in your own work-life experience.

Is the company solely responsible for motivating its employees, or do employees themselves also have a responsibility in this regard?

Many companies today have implemented motivational reward schemes involving peer-to-peer rewards and recognition sentiments. In such schemes, employees can reward their colleagues even when there is no official reporting line between them. These rewards are often implemented via online systems; for example, providing the opportunity to send a thank you message via the company intranet to a colleague who has done a job well.

In some systems, other employees are able to read these messages. This can be seen as a virtual "pat on the back" and can provide important visible recognition across the company. These incentives form part of a gamified approach to rewards and recognition. When points are awarded as part of a recognition, they can be redeemed for gifts from a company website.

An awesome responsibility

Barry-Wehmiller is a multi-billion-dollar manufacturing company that makes packaging machinery and other materials. During the economic crisis of 2008, the company experienced a precipitous drop in orders from its customers. It quickly became apparent that there was not enough revenue to justify paying all of the employees.

Bob Chapman, Barry-Wehmiller's CEO since 1975, began to consider the possibility of layoffs but quickly dismissed the idea. He said that the company's vision of success was about more than financial performance. Chapman considers the employees at Barry-Wehmiller to be a family so he asked himself, what would a family do? The answer was obvious: A family would share the burden.

Thus, instead of laying off some employees with devastating consequences to them, Chapman and his executive team decided that the company's response would be one of shared sacrifice. Everyone would be required to take unpaid leave for four weeks in the year. Barry-Wehmiller also stopped matching contributions to its employees' retirement plans. Throughout, the company communicated regularly with its employees, updating them on the state of the business, what was being done and why, and reassuring people that the future was secure.

The reaction was overwhelmingly positive. Everyone pulled together to get through a difficult period. Some people even offered to take eight weeks of unpaid leave to compensate for their colleagues who could not afford to take four weeks. After the crisis had passed, Barry-Wehmiller recorded three consecutive years of record profits, reinstated the matching contributions to retirement plans and even paid employees back what they would have received had the matching programme not been stopped.

Bob Chapman says that in return for how it responded to the economic crisis, Barry-Wehmiller's employees repaid the company with something truly priceless: their trust. His philosophy of business is elegantly summed up in a quote on his profile page on the company's website: "Business could be the most powerful force for good in the world, if leaders would embrace the awesome responsibility of leadership. Caring for people and giving them meaning, purpose, and fulfillment through their work is not in disharmony with creating value."

Managing the team

Managers play an important role when it comes to providing motivation for their team. It is important that managers be able to define their vision and key objectives and to articulate them in a way that brings the team along with them. Great managers have the ability to get their teams to go further together than they could have ever gone alone.

Carlos Folguera is the former head of "La Masia" FC Barcelona, one of the most successful football (soccer) clubs of all time. La Masia is the name of the home where the elite youth of FC Barcelona are trained and prepared for the potential of playing top-flight football for one of the greatest clubs in the world.

The players who make it are destined to become superstars and many of them go on to become celebrities with huge earning power. Carlos explained that in the world of professional football, you cannot use conventional methods of motivation, such as salary and bonuses. Some of these players are earning more money than they can imagine, and they are already seen as superstars by the media and their millions of fans. So how do you motivate them?

Carlos said that his job as a manager is to help to create a culture of well-being, self-improvement, and respect among the players so that they work hard for each other and hold each other accountable. He did this by establishing one key value which formed the DNA of the club, "respect for each other." Then they invested time in demonstrating what respect for each other looked and felt like both on and off the pitch. As part of their personal development, each member of La Masia must define what respect means to him and how he can show it to others.

The role of the manager of any team is, or should be, one of co-creation. A great manager takes the time to get to know the team members and works to create an environment where they can thrive as a team.

Think back to school and your favorite subject. Was that subject taught, coincidentally, by one of your favorite teachers? Did they have the ability to make the subject exciting and relevant for you? If so, you probably showed up to class fully motivated and ready to learn regardless of the difficulty of the lesson. This is the art of great employer–employee relationship development.

Motivation in your workplace

You have already done a fair amount of work in this chapter on the things that motivate you, but there is one additional step. It will help you gain clarity about work-related motivators and the alignment (or misalignment) with the things that motivate you. It will help ensure that your approach to your work life motivates you in a meaningful way. Any gaps will be the starting point for you to create a plan to establish or restore the alignment.

EXERCISE: Gaps in motivation

On the scrolls on the next page, write down examples of the ways in which your company motivates employees. It does not matter how trivial the examples are. For example, does it organize regular coffee meetings for teams to get together? Is there a company car policy or a year-end bonus scheme? Does the company provide free meals or drinks?

Now ask yourself, what motivates you? You captured some of the areas of motivation that are important to you in an earlier exercise on page 75. Now be as specific as possible and take the time to go into more detail.

Looking at these two lists, link those areas of personal motivation with the range of company initiatives that are directly related to your areas of interest. For example, if time affluence is an important motivator for you, and your company allows people to work flex time, you would link the two.

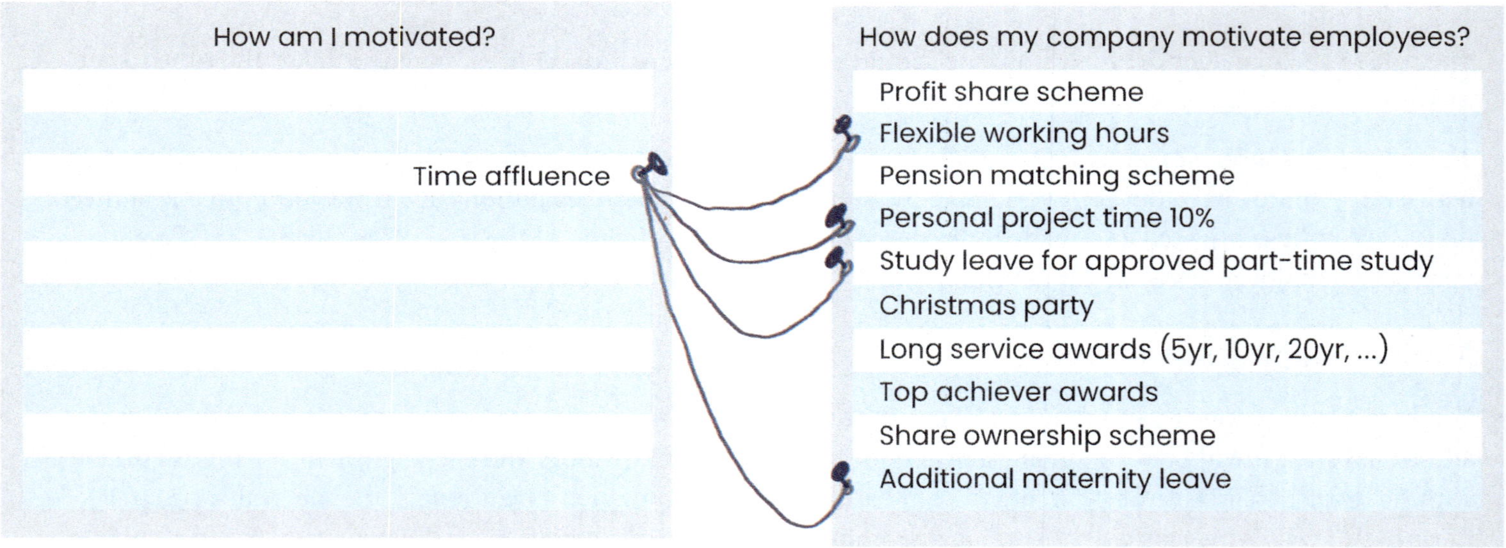

Now look at the gaps, if any, between the areas of motivation that are important to you and how the company is meeting them. Are there things that would motivate you that the company is not doing? Do you see any examples where a stronger alignment could be established between your motivation triggers and those offered in your workplace?

It is important that you have a clear understanding of the things that motivate you about your work, your colleagues, and your company. You will be able to use this awareness to cultivate your own personal checklist to ensure that you maintain a healthy motivation in your work life.

How am I motivated?
How does my company motivate employees?

Your values in action

If we now start to dig deeper, what is it that guides your decisions to pursue certain goals but to avoid others? What are the characteristics and behaviors that help you to consciously choose and act in a certain manner to satisfy your desires? This is where you start to identify and focus on your personal values.

A value is a conscious choice to act in a certain way. Your values are the fundamental beliefs that you decide are important to guide and motivate your behavior as well as the choices you make about what is important in your life.

Note that there is a difference between the things that you value and your actual personal values. For example, maybe financial wealth is something that you value, but how you get it matters; a decision to mastermind a bank robbery to achieve financial wealth probably indicates a questionable set of personal values. We hope that instead, you believe that "honesty is the best policy" and seek to achieve financial wealth legally and honorably.

Identifying your personal values can, at first, be challenging. However, once you have done so, you can establish guidelines on how to use these to make conscious decisions about the things that motivate you and the goals that you put in place to satisfy your desires. They also influence how you proceed to carry them out. Your personal values define your character, which is how you behave when nobody is watching. Your personal values define you.

Escape from Silicon Valley

Irene worked as an IT manager for a large company in Silicon Valley where she was responsible for a team of fifty programmers. When she began her career, job security was very important. She believed that she would find security in a job with a recognized multinational company that offered a good salary and great prospects. Irene enjoyed the opportunities the company provided and for many years did not question her drivers.

Over time, however, Irene realized that her desire to feel safe prevented her from feeling aligned with her personal values such as freedom, connectedness, and the possibility to innovate and discover new insights. She was no longer happy in her "secure" job, which she realized after having been through several restructurings, was not so secure after all.

Irene understood that she needed to overcome her fears in order to live in alignment with her true self. She had to find an environment in which she could experiment and share insights on innovative projects with people with whom she felt connected. Such opportunities were limited in her multinational company.

It took Irene a long time to overcome her fears, which resulted in her staying at the same company for twenty years. Eventually, she made a change.

Today, Irene runs her own consultancy company. She travels the world and still works with multinationals, but now she can select the projects that interest her and that provide her with the room to express her ideas. Her clients value her work and she feels safe and happy in her new world.

It's all about you

Your personal values are unique to you. They are a product of your upbringing, your experiences, and your social circles. They are a description of your character, your behavior, your likes, and your dislikes. Most importantly, your personal values hold true no matter what, even in times of stress and temptation.

However, your personal values are not immutable; they can evolve and change over time. It is important to remain aware of your values throughout your life and to make the necessary adjustments as they change so that you continue to live in accordance with them as best you can, even if there are times when they might be threatened or compromised.

Sadly, most people do not take the time to work on this fundamental tenet of their life. This results in a staggering number of people who consider their jobs as being less than ideal. They end up making decisions that are not in harmony with their personal values and end up regretting the choices that have been made.

So, it is helpful to think about your personal values and to question how they were established. Did they serve you once, but today they now hold you back? Did you take them from someone else but they no longer have a place in your life? Many of us are being guided by values that were given to us by friends, parents, relatives, bosses, and the media.

There is a common misconception that to connect with your inner self and identify your personal values, it is necessary to go to an isolated location in the mountains, on an island, or in a desert. Most of us don't have this option, but the good news is that you can work on connecting to your personal values wherever you are.

Just for the health of it

Peter likes to be fit and healthy. When he maintains a regular fitness regime and eats well, he feels good. He can concentrate well at work; he has clarity in his thoughts and feels energized. He sleeps well and has a positive outlook on life. When he is with his friends and colleagues, he is always in good humor and enjoys the company of others.

However, if there are periods when Peter is unable to exercise regularly, or if he is unable to eat well, he does not feel so good. In these situations, his motivation starts to wane and he feels sluggish. He becomes irritable with others when confronted with difficult situations and the positive feelings that he normally has when times are good start to disappear.

Considering this scenario, Peter might decide to believe that health and fitness are important personal values. With this belief, he proactively tries to maintain a healthy diet and exercise. Practically, this means that he avoids eating junk food and monitors his weight and overall health. He does not sit for long periods of time at his computer and takes regular breaks. He also ensures that he continues with his exercise regime as a priority.

Peter keeps these personal values in the forefront of his mind when making decisions about what to do or not to do. The feeling of well-being that results from the choices made in alignment with his personal values are important to him.

Exercise: Your personal values

Take some time to think about your own personal values. What is important to you? Are there any "lines in the sand" that you will not cross? How do you feel in situations where your values are threatened or under pressure? These situations can be related to your personal or work life.

It might be helpful to refer to the examples of motivation that you explored earlier on. How did it feel when you were motivated to work towards achieving a certain goal? How did it feel when you succeeded or failed? Why are these feelings so important to you, either to seek them or to avoid them? Does it matter how you achieve your goals? Do you care about what other people think about you when you are working to meet your goals?

For each of the personal values that you identify, complete the following sentences:

- I decide to believe that ______________________________ is a personal value of mine.
- This personal value is important to me because ______________________________.
- When I act according to this personal value, I feel ______________________________.
- When I do not act according to this personal value, I feel ______________________________.

Place your values around the ship's wheel on the next page.

My personal values

To assist you with this exercise, let us take the example above of Peter who wants to be fit and healthy. He completes the four sentences above as follows:

Thinking about others

Another way to help you identify your personal values is to think about the people in your life whom you admire for the values by which they live. The values we hold most dear are typically personified in people whom we admire and love. When we admire a quality in others it is usually an indication of something that we value ourselves or something to which we aspire.

EXERCISE: Your role models

On the chart above, write down the names of people whom you admire. They can be people you know personally or not; they may be alive, or they may have lived centuries ago. For each person, list four personal values that you believe that person embodies.

Consider each of the values that you have listed and consider if these values are also important for you. If so, add them to your list and complete the sentences on page 92, as you did for your initial values that you identified.

What do these exercises reveal? What are the personal values that help you decide whom you spend your time with? With which projects do you choose to get involved? For which company do you decide to work?

Your personal values can act as a metaphorical "line in the sand" that you are not willing to cross because it would go against something that is fundamentally important to who you are as a person. Are you willing to make compromises? How would you feel if you did?

From these exercises you should have a clearer idea of your personal values. If you need further help to test the validity of the values that you have chosen, consider the following questions for each value:

- Would you sacrifice this personal value for money?
- Have you been in a situation when you have not lived up to this personal value in a time of stress?
- If you were in a competitive situation (e.g., applying for a promotion), would you ignore this personal value if it would put you in an advantageous position?

If you answer "yes" to any of these questions for any of your personal values, reconsider whether you really have a strong commitment and belief in those values.

Ultimately, only you will know if you have truly lived according to your personal values.

Your frame of reference

Everyone is different; everyone is unique. However, defending our uniqueness is an ongoing effort as the world—family, school, work—constantly works to get us to conform. As the writer and philosopher Ralph Waldo Emerson said, "To be yourself in a world that is constantly trying to change you is the greatest accomplishment."

As you have worked through the topics and exercises in this book thus far, one thing should be clear. Your frame is unique to you. How you take yourself to work, interact and connect with your colleagues, and how you are motivated and guided by your personal values are all unique. This might seem obvious, but do not lose sight of this fact as you move into the next phase of your journey.

In the following two chapters, you will start to focus on specific areas of your work life that you would like to explore and develop further. Some of these topics will be familiar to you but others might be discoveries.

To take full advantage of this next stage of your journey, it is important not to be constrained by your current frame. We will reference it in a constructive way. You might even decide to explore topics that are currently not in your frame. That is perfectly OK. You will be guided along the way.

PART TWO

FOCUS

CHAPTER FOUR

From Little Acorns

"It is never too late to be who you might have been."
– George Eliot

Coming into focus

Thus far, you have explored your attitude toward your work and how connected you feel in the workplace. You have also explored your motivations and values.

These elements define the frame for your current work-life context. This frame is the foundation upon which you will now start to focus on areas that are important for you to develop further to become the best possible version of you. You will explore and discover new insights into your unique talents and how to derive maximum fulfillment and happiness from those talents.

The old English proverb, "Mighty oaks from little acorns grow" dates back to the fourteenth Century. It means that, with time, things that are small and modest can become big and impressive. This proverb has significance for many aspects of our everyday lives. It can inspire us to remember that great achievements stem from humble beginnings. It can also help us to keep things in perspective by thinking about the long term.

An oak tree does not become mighty overnight. It must go through different stages of development and growth, each of which is necessary to enable the tree to reach its full potential. For a tree to become mighty, it needs strong roots, the proper environment, good weather, fertile soil, and an ecosystem in which it can thrive. Even if a tree goes through traumatic experiences during its lifetime, those experiences can often make it stronger and more resilient.

Look at the trees

The next time you go for a walk in nature, notice the trees. Some are tall and majestic, others are small. Some are deciduous and others are conifers. Some are in hostile environments, hidden from the sun by taller trees, others live on soil with hardly any nutrition. Some have survived fire or flood or wind. They all stand and continue to grow. It does not matter what species they are, whether they are part of a forest or standing alone. Each tree is beautiful in its own way.

How do these wonders of nature relate to your work life? Do you have years of experience or are you just starting out on your career? Do you work with others or alone? Are you in a friendly or hostile environment? Have you had to deal with unexpected challenges?

As you reflect on these questions, think about the possibilities that are open to you, acknowledge the difficulties you have faced to make it this far. Think about the future and all that it has to offer as you grow and develop.

Just as all trees start from tiny seeds, we all start from somewhere. As we grow, the fruits of our development bring us successes and failures, opportunities and challenges. Ultimately, we should want to develop into the best possible version of ourselves.

Like a tree, your development is unique and might not be linear. From your personal starting point, you might experience several twists along the way to reaching your full potential. Prior to picking up this book, you have had successes and failures. You overcame some challenges and were thwarted by others. You have had fulfilling and unfulfilling experiences. There have been times when you showed resilience and times when you gave up.

It is all part of your journey.

As you continue to work through this book, you will now explore in more detail some of the key elements from your current frame and create a focus on potential outcomes and development paths that you want to take. Let's look at what development means to you and why it is important in your life.

It all begins at, well, the beginning.

Know thyself

Your initial development was shaped by the education that you received from your family and your school.

Perhaps you had role models in your family and followed their path. Or perhaps you had a different reaction and you ran in the opposite direction, determined to do anything *but* what the people around you did. As for school, how much choice did you have in what you studied? Did you follow a standard curriculum?

Although an academic degree is valuable, it provides no guarantees for professional success, fulfillment, or happiness, especially if, as the British education specialist Sir Ken Robinson said, "it marginalizes what you think is important about yourself." How much did your education help you to express your uniqueness? How well did it prepare you for a fulfilling professional life?

If your education did not help you in identifying your individual needs and aspirations, take heart. You are not alone. The academic and business worlds have long focused on giving you the elements required for a traditional success model, which says you will be successful once you achieve a certain status or position in your work life. Many people will say that you become someone by virtue of what you accumulate: diplomas; positions; promotions; money; material objects.

What if you do not fit this model of success? Does it mean that you are not successful? Is this the right standard by which to measure your development, your happiness, your fulfillment? We don't think so.

Now is the moment to focus and take a deeper look at what lies inside of you. The Latin maxim *temet nosce* (know thyself) is as relevant today as it was centuries ago. You must know who you are before you can decide where you want to go and who you want to be.

Your development—a work in progress

Just as there are no two trees with the same growth path, your development is unique. It is about your needs, your potential, your knowledge, your environment, your aspirations, and your skills.

There are many aspects to your development in your work life. It includes formal development activities such as training courses, academic studies, guidance from mentors, and self-learning. But it is more than that. It also includes your experiences, good and bad. It can come from successes as well as failures. Indeed, any experience is part of your development.

Your strengths

You already know a lot about yourself, from what you look like in the morning to the kind of music that you enjoy. But if you are to develop, you must know yourself deeply.

Moving beyond your current frame requires a better understanding of your unique development path. It starts by understanding the intersection between what you are naturally good at and what you love to do.

People feel more confident, self-aware, and productive when they focus on their strengths. When you work in an environment where you can use your strengths, you feel motivated and energized because you see how your strengths make an impact. When you focus on your strengths, you will also find more opportunities to grow.

In his book, *The Element*, Sir Ken Robinson took this notion one step further. He wrote that when you reach the point at which natural talent meets personal passion, you will be in your element. By finding and nurturing your element, you can ignite your creativity and bring more vitality and passion to your life and to the world.

There's something about Mary

Mary worked in the marketing department for a large technology company that provides IT solutions for small and large enterprises. She worked closely with a global sales team responsible for large corporations.

Mary was passionate about finding creative solutions for her customers by working with her colleagues in the marketing and sales departments and she excelled at listening to people. People loved getting her perspective when facing a complex situation. Mary listened to them and asked good questions. Together, they always came up with great solutions.

After many years working in marketing, Mary felt that her contributions didn't match her ambitions anymore. It was hard for her to stay engaged in her job and she felt that she needed a new challenge. Her manager had told her that she would be a great fit for a sales role, but Mary did not see how her skills would help her to be successful as a salesperson.

Eventually, Mary did accept a sales role. As expected, there were several aspects of sales that she had to learn. However, she also found that her deep understanding of the technology and her capability to listen and ask smart questions were key to her success. Mary realized that she could see her existing skills and passion in a new light and use them to have a successful and rewarding sales job. It was a terrific growth opportunity.

Years later, Mary confidently founded her own marketing consulting firm and specialized in working with small companies that sell technology. Combining her marketing, sales experience, and capacity to find solutions to complex problems made her a very successful entrepreneur.

EXERCISE: Your strengths and your passions

In the first column of the table below, list all of the things that you are good at, even if you do not like doing them. In the second column, list all of the things that you love to do, regardless of whether you are good at them or not. The activities in either column can be related to your work or not.

Here are some questions on which you can reflect before you begin:

- What kinds of problems can you most easily solve?
- In what areas do you naturally excel?
- What positive feedback do you regularly receive?
- What energizes you?

Write down whatever comes to mind. If something fits in each column, put it in both.

What I am good at	What I love to do

Now that you have completed the table, let's go deeper.

Are there things that you are good at *and* that you love to do? How often do you do them? In which context or situations do you do them?

What I am good at and love to do	**Context or situation**

Are there things that you love to do, but which you are *not* good at? How can you improve?

What I love to do but am not good at	**How I can improve**

Finally, are there things that you are good at, but which you do *not* love to do? What could you do about these types of situations? Could you stop doing the activity? Could you make an adjustment that would change your attitude? Do you even want to change your attitude (because sometimes you don't and that is fine)?

What I am good at but do not love	**Changes I could make**

These exercises will give you a high-level picture of your strengths and passions. This knowledge can be a game changer for your career and your life. Your strengths and passions are your superpowers, and they help you create a life that you love.

After doing these exercises, you might be more attentive to the things that you love to do and have renewed energy for them. You might be motivated to improve and could even discover new ways at work in which to apply the things that you love.

Write down any insights that you have. They might be related to what you want to focus on, what is missing and what you want to remove. Perhaps your insights will reveal patterns that are related to a bigger picture.

All that is possible

Aspirations can be thought of as overarching life goals that can provide you with a sense of purpose and direction. As the English writer Samuel Johnson said, "Your aspirations are your possibilities." Although the word "aspirations" is often used synonymously with "goals," there are some important differences.

Goals tend to be backed by actions and are often, though not always, focused on the near future. Aspirations, on the other hand, tend to be focused on the long term. They are something with which you feel an emotional connection and can stretch for years if not an entire lifetime.

In the following pages, we invite you to dream big and to think about how your goals and a spirations will enable you to make a meaningful impact in the world.

Deeper than skin deep

Alex was born in the former Yugoslavia in the early 1970s. His father was from Ghana and his mother was from what is now Slovenia.

Alex's dark skin was extremely rare in Yugoslavia at that time and he was often in the middle of fights and struggles because of it. Had it not been for his courage and tenacity, Alex would probably have developed into a quiet person who avoided conflict.

At an early age, Alex recognized that people in conflicting situations focus on their differences rather than what they have in common. Growing up, he became more and more interested in finding solutions to conflicts by helping people overcome their differences, showing them the bigger picture and creating a platform where differences could be resolved in a way that respected the values of all parties.

Driven by his strengths in communication, his ability to adapt quickly to changing situations, and his high level of sensitivity, Alex became a successful lawyer and an advisor to the Slovenian government.

He vividly remembers the satisfaction of creating unexpected partnerships between institutions that seemed very different, but that in fact had the same goal. By helping these institutions to understand the bigger goal, and by encouraging each side to approach the solution with curiosity towards the other, Alex was able to move things forward.

It was only by looking backwards over his life and "connecting the dots" between his childhood conflicts and his career path, that Alex has been able to articulate his overarching aspiration in life. He puts it this way:

> "I firmly believe that humanity can only evolve when we learn to recognize and leverage our differences instead of fighting them. My mission is to open people's eyes to alternatives, broaden their perspectives and encourage them to appreciate their differences so that we can create communities driven by curiosity and understanding."

This bold statement is much more than a yearly goal; it is an aspiration that governs Alex's professional and personal life. It allows him to feel energized to continue his journey. By articulating his aspiration, Alex also feels that it is easier to set priorities and to say no to the things that do not support it.

Thinking differently about aspirations

When you think of your aspirations, don't limit yourself to career-related aspirations. It is not about the typical question you get asked in job interviews or from your managers such as where you see yourself in five years or what your next professional goal is.

In today's world, the distinction between one's personal and professional life has become blurred. More and more people recognize that it is possible to have careers that match personal needs. So, we need to look at aspirations differently. Aspirations relate to the long-term dreams that you are pursuing. They are your vision for your future, and they are deeply connected to the impact that you want to make.

Your strengths and passions have a role to play as you explore your aspirations. This is why you enjoy doing the things you do and why you are attracted to strengthen certain areas.

Thinking about aspirations goes beyond just seeing a future state of your current strengths and passions or thinking about a future job challenge. There is a need to think about them in terms of the impact that you seek to create. This introspection starts from your conviction that some things must change so that your world can become a better place.

Defining your aspirations

At this point you have gathered your insights about your values, motivations, strengths, and what you love doing. Take some time to reflect on your findings. As you start to formulate your aspirations, allow yourself to dream big and be bold. Now, use the table below to capture your ideas.

EXERCISE: Your aspirations

Your aspirations

What changes do I want to see in my world?	How can I contribute?	Why do I believe these changes are needed?	Who needs these changes?	How will my contribution be valued?

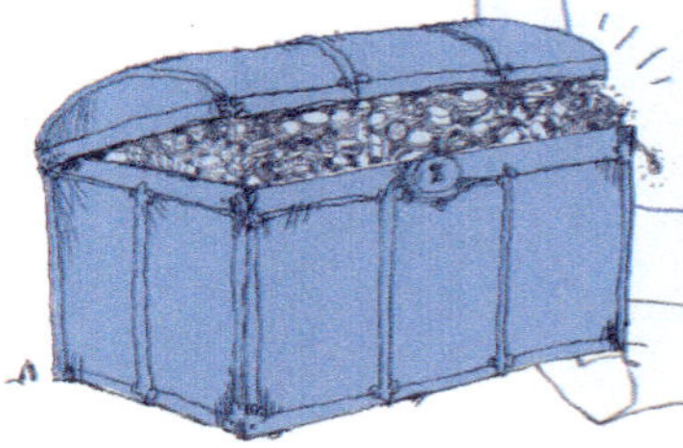

By answering these questions, you will start to see what you want to change and why. You will discover what to do to make that change, and what the impact will be.

Consider each of these elements in more detail:

1. What changes do you want to see in your world?

Do you want to challenge the status quo in some way? Do you want to make the world better in some specific way? Reflect on your life so far. Are there any connections between the things that you have done and the changes that you want to make?

You might find it helpful to refer to the tables above where you listed the things that you love to do. Is there a pattern that provides clues as to what changes you seek?

2. How can you contribute?

You need to consider what will make it possible for you to make a meaningful contribution to bring about your desired changes. Think about your strengths and experience, and how you can use them to create the impact you seek. Refer to the exercise above on strengths.

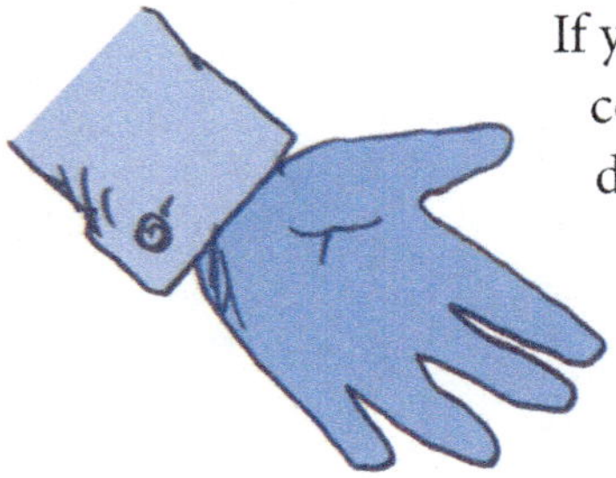

If you lack certain skills or resources to make a meaningful contribution, note them down; you will add them to your development plan and journey.

When you are passionate about something and you have some of the strengths to allow you to make your desired impact, whatever is missing can be developed or complemented with the help of others.

3. Why do you believe these changes are needed?

You probably have strong reasons why the changes that you seek are necessary. Think about the consequences of those changes. What would be different in the world if they were to happen? What problems would those changes solve?

4. Who needs these changes?

To make your aspirations tangible, think about the people (or things) that will benefit from the change. Who will care about your contribution? Be as precise as possible. You do not need to impact the entire world for your impact to be meaningful.

5. How will your contribution be valued?

Think about the value that will flow from the realization of your aspiration. How will you and others recognize this value? Who will acknowledge, share, or even pay for it?

Once you have a few ideas in each column you might be ready to formulate your aspiration. Review what you have written in each of the columns. Do you see an overarching theme, something that connects your answers? If not, don't worry. Just follow the ideas row by row and do your best to bring them together.

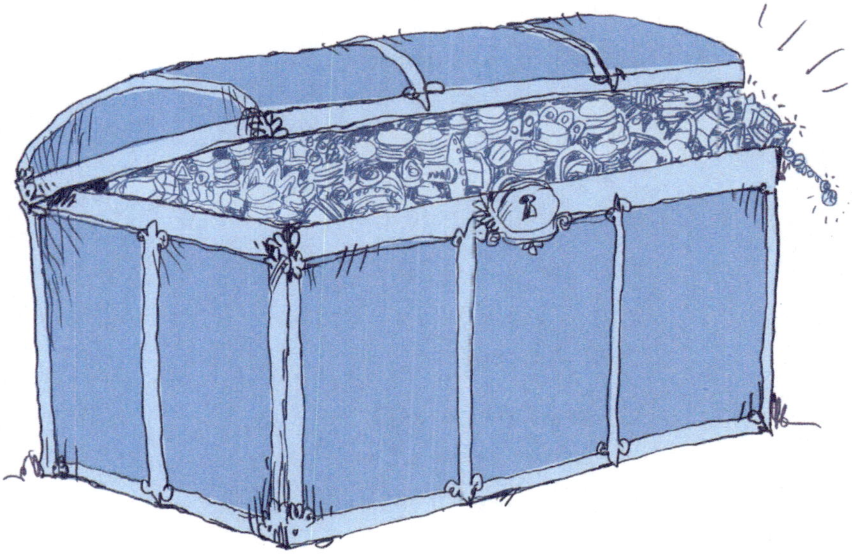

A concrete example might help stimulate your thinking. Do you remember the story of Alex on page 112? As a reminder, this was his aspiration:

> "I firmly believe that humanity can only evolve when we learn to recognize and leverage our differences instead of fighting them. My mission is to open people's eyes to alternatives, broaden their perspectives and encourage them to appreciate their differences so that we can create communities driven by curiosity and understanding."

Let's see what Alex wrote in the columns when he was working on his aspiration. For Alex, there was a clear, overarching theme. He had a clear idea of the change that was needed, how he could help and who would benefit.

What changes do I want to see in my world?

Break through the impasse of current polarization and numbness

Transform media, politics, and business

Opponents find common ground and realize there is a bigger, common context for them

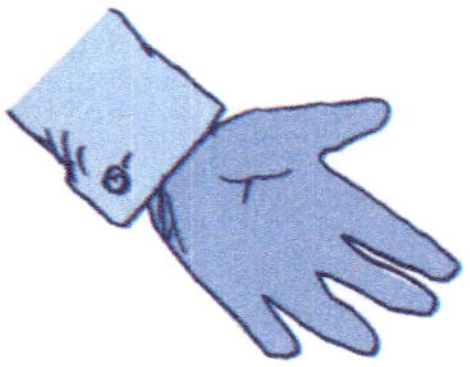

How can I contribute?

Make people see more, think more, question more, so they can be better, smarter, and empowered (vs lost, overwhelmed, and scared)

Provide context for people and empower them to appreciate their differences

Open people's eyes to alternative perspectives and broader considerations

Why do I believe these changes are needed?

So that society can advance into the next level

So that people realize the potential that lies in the collective, which is greater than the sum of the individuals

So that communities switch from fighting to understanding

Who needs these changes?

People in communities who believe there must be a better way but who do not think they can do anything about it

How will my contribution be valued?

Mediation services to create partnerships between institutions and communities

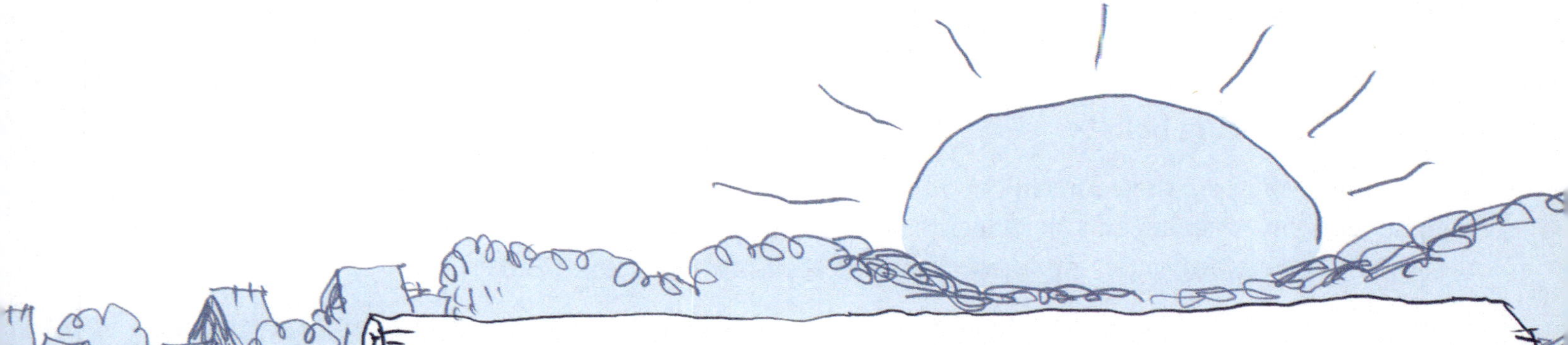

It might take a few iterations to go through these questions before your aspirations come into focus. If so, take your time. Work on answering the questions for a while and then take a break. Come back to them later with fresh eyes and see what new ideas evolve. However long it takes, the more precise you can be, the better.

You will know that you have found the answer when:

- It comes from your heart. You feel it and others who know you immediately recognize you in your aspiration statement when they hear it.
- It is short and clear. You do not have to explain it. Even strangers will understand it.
- It is inspiring. It is something that is bigger than you and it stirs emotion in others.

Limiting beliefs are your kryptonite

Your strengths and passions may be your superpowers, but like every superhero, you are not invulnerable. Superman may have had incredible strength, X-ray vision, and the ability to fly, but put a piece of kryptonite anywhere near him and you could beat him in an arm-wrestling match. Like Superman, you have your own metaphorical kryptonite: your limiting beliefs.

A limiting belief is a negative thought that has become embedded in your mind. It is a conviction that you believe is true and that limits you in some way.

For example, in the story on page 107, Mary thought that she could never be a salesperson. It was not because of her sales skills—she was extremely competent—but because she had a limiting belief about herself and what she was capable of doing. Quite simply, Mary believed that she was not good at selling. Fortunately for Mary, she was able to overcome her limiting beliefs. You can too, but you must identify and understand them before you can break them.

The roots of limiting beliefs

Many limiting beliefs are rooted in childhood experiences. We create our own rules from an early age through events, observations, and the influence of others. These beliefs often begin with family-imposed rules, values, and actions. Later, they come from education and work experiences.

We then translate these experiences into ideas, feelings, and beliefs. These beliefs, in turn, influence our decisions about how we engage with others, which career we choose and how we behave. What about you?

It is important to understand your limiting beliefs and make them part of your development journey. If you do not deal with them correctly, they will have a negative impact on the decisions you make, and ultimately, whether you are able to reach your full potential.

Admitting and understanding your limiting beliefs is not easy, but it is critical to your development.

Identifying your limiting beliefs

When you think of your limiting beliefs, you might already have some specific examples in mind. There are four main types of limiting beliefs. They relate to your skills, your character, your interactions with others, and your understanding of the world.

Some examples are as follows:

- Skills: "I am not good at ______________________________."

- Character: "I lack the courage to ____."

- Interactions with others: "I do not know how to ______________________________________ with people."

- Understanding of the world: "In order to ______________________________, I must first ____."
- Understanding of the world: "Most people working in this sector are ______________________________, so I would not be a good fit for this job."

Take a few minutes now to reflect on situations or experiences in which you felt uncomfortable, fearful, or inadequate. What is it about the situation or experience that made you feel that way? These negative feelings may be attached to some limiting beliefs.

EXERCISE: Your limiting beliefs

Based on your reflection, note your thoughts and ideas about your limiting beliefs on the scrolls below.

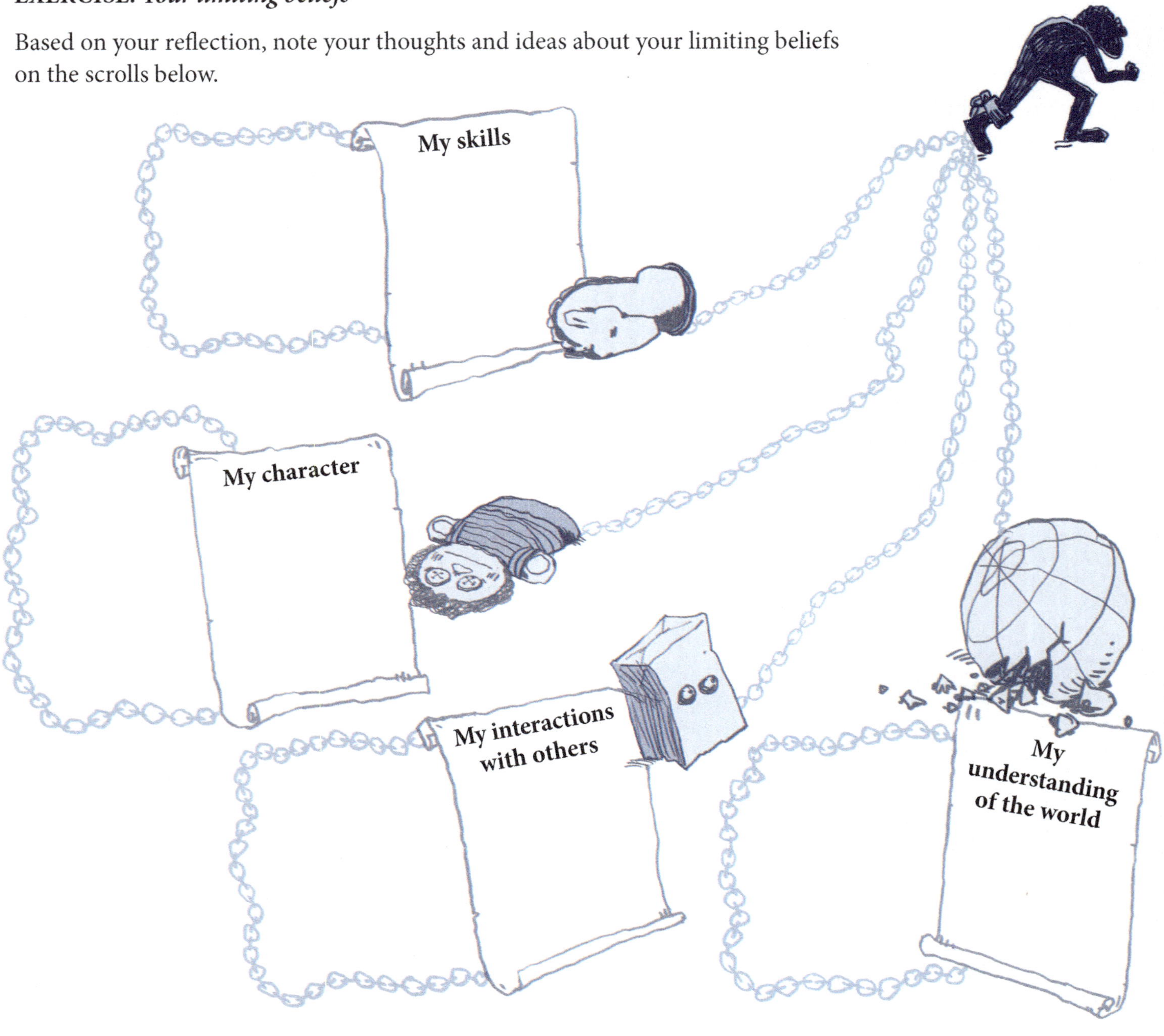

Once you have completed the scrolls above, you should go back to the tables that you created starting on page 108 about the things that you are good at and the things that you love to do. Look at those things that you love to do but are not good at and add them to the scrolls above if they are not already there.

Breaking your limiting beliefs

As counterintuitive as it might seem, you must begin the process of breaking your limiting beliefs by going in the opposite direction and make those beliefs stronger!

EXERCISE: Supporting arguments for your limiting beliefs

Pick one of your limiting beliefs. Why do you think that limiting belief is true? Write out each supporting argument in the following way: "I am not good at X because [reason 1]. I am not good at X because [reason 2]," etc.

Write down every possible supporting argument. Even if they sound ridiculous to you, do not discard them. They are still the supporting arguments for your limiting beliefs, and they must be uprooted one by one.

Let's take a concrete example. Go back to page 107 and read Mary's story again. Even though Mary's manager had suggested sales as a great opportunity for her, Mary believed that she was not good at selling. Her supporting arguments were:

- I am not good at selling because sales are all about convincing and I am not persuasive.
- I am not good at selling because I am a woman and the tech world is a man's world.
- I am not good at selling because I am not pushy.
- I am not good at selling because it is all about networking and I am not good at it.

Once you have your limiting beliefs with their supporting arguments, it is time to uproot those arguments. Go through each one. Is it possible that your supporting arguments are incorrect? Are there things that you might not know? Are you making any false assumptions?

EXERCISE: Counterarguments

Let's work with one of Mary's arguments supporting her limiting belief about her ability to sell. Mary thinks that because she is a woman, she will not be good at sales because men dominate the tech world. But is it really true that women cannot be good salespeople in the tech world?

What about women like Marissa Mayer, former President and CEO of Yahoo!, or Sheryl Sandberg, former COO of Meta? They had to be able to sell—ideas, projects, concepts—in order to be successful. What about the thousands of women doing important sales work at large, medium, and small tech companies around the world?

Let's have Mary go deeper. Her own manager said that sales would be a great fit for her. Why did she doubt him? Did she think that he was just being nice? Has she ever discussed her skills at selling with her colleagues, friends, or family? Has she ever asked for feedback? Has she investigated the career paths of women who have been successful in sales?

By taking the time to reflect on the above questions, Mary began to realize that her supporting argument about women in sales in tech was not as strong as she had thought.

What about you? Now that you have gone through your supporting arguments for your limiting beliefs, are they as strong as you previously thought? Have you discovered cracks in the foundations of these supporting arguments? Are any of them now obviously wrong?

The next step in the process is to come up with counterarguments for each reason supporting your limiting belief. Continuing with Mary, let's look at some counterarguments to her supporting argument about women in tech.

- Many women have been successful in the tech world.
- The women who have reached the top of their profession in the tech world had to have been good at selling ideas to others.
- Selling is about persuasive communication and that is something that women can do as well as men.
- My manager believes in me and would not have suggested sales if he did not think that I was capable of doing a great job.
- Based on feedback that I have received from others, I do have skills that would be beneficial to selling. I can work on those skills and get better at them.

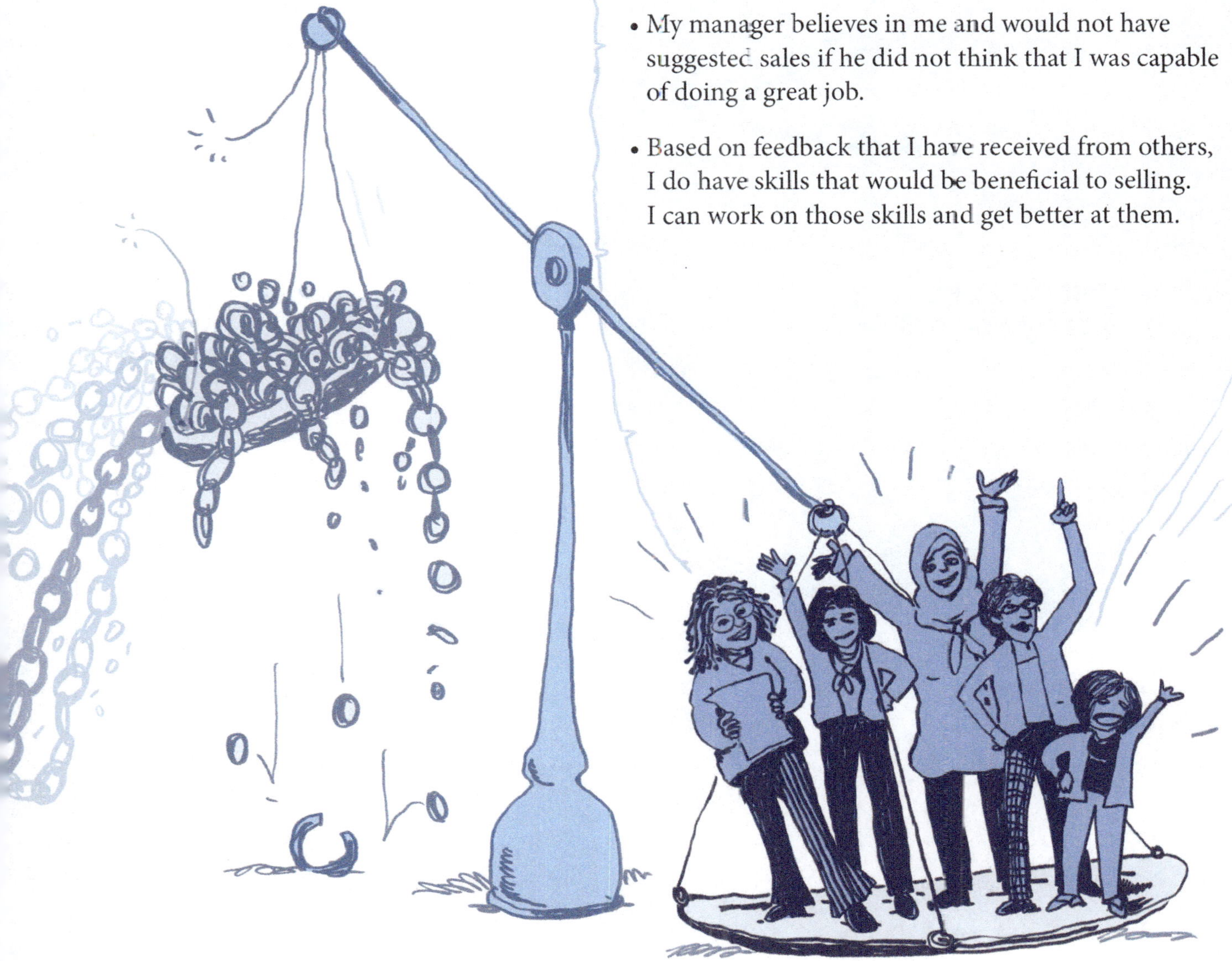

Now it's your turn. For each argument that supports your limiting belief, write out as many counterarguments as possible.

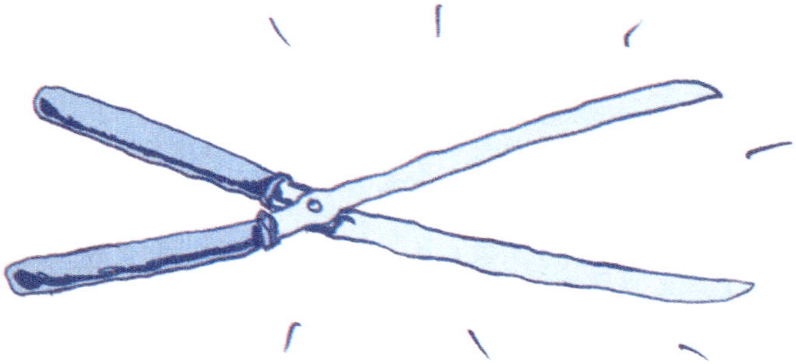

Arguments supporting the limiting belief	Counterarguments

At the end of this exercise, you should be able to put the arguments supporting your limiting belief into one of two groups: (a) those that are wrong, whether based on faulty assumptions or a lack of information; and (b) those that are true but that you can change by working on them. It is this second group on which you must now concentrate.

When Mary worked on her supporting argument—that women cannot be successful in sales in the tech world—she realized that many women have indeed been successful in this regard. She further realized that she did have skills that would serve her well in a sales position. Admittedly, she needed to improve some of those skills. However, she had several options for doing so such as books, training programs, and mentorship. By working on her skills, as we read earlier, Mary became very successful.

Tackling the arguments that support your limiting beliefs will require commitment and action on your part. In some cases, you will be able to make progress quickly; in others, it might be a process that lasts months or even years.

Take note of these arguments because you will do some further reflection on how your aspiration could become a reality by tapping into who you already are, and by finding your authentic voice.

The way forward

Thus far, you have defined key elements of your current frame context. You have reflected on the things that you discovered about your values, strengths, development needs, and aspirations.

You also did the challenging work of facing and assessing your limiting beliefs and what must be done to overcome them. Your limiting beliefs are a fundamental part of your journey because they can prevent you from achieving your longer-term aspirations if they are not addressed. They are key areas of personal development for you to work on.

It won't always be easy. Along the way, there will be obstacles and challenges. You will have to deal with them in order to successfully continue your journey and achieve fulfillment and happiness.

Take some time to appreciate the work that you have done thus far. With every exercise, with every reflection, this book transforms a bit more into your personal Journey Map. Stay with it for a while and reflect on how you are feeling about it and what you have learned about yourself. By investing the time to do these exercises, have you learned anything new? Have you found answers to some of the questions which you have been asking yourself?

At the beginning of this chapter, we quoted the English novelist, George Eliot, who said that it is never too late to be who you might have been. When thinking about your journey thus far, you might catch a glimpse of the person you could have been ... and still can be.

Heading in the right direction

Now that you understand your aspirations more clearly, it is possible that you are already well on your way to achieving them. Alternatively, they might still just be dreams that you want to turn into realities.

In either case, what will it take to bring your aspirations to life? How will things change when you can truly show up as yourself, be open about your aspirations, and bring your ideas to the world?

To start, share your plans with someone whom you trust and who could be a partner in your journey. It could be a friend, spouse, or even your manager. See if your aspirations resonate with them and ask for feedback. Telling others about your plans can help with your commitment to act on it.

At times, you will be encouraged by your progress. At other times, you will experience roadblocks and frustration. It is all part of the process. There will be zig zags, detours, and dead ends along the way, but there will also be steps (sometimes leaps) forward. And there will be joy and disappointment. However, as you progress, whenever you experience a roadblock or a difficulty on your path, you will see more ways to overcome them with the help of experts, friends, like-minded people, and even through your own self-development. It will become natural to be on a continuous journey of self-development.

With time, you will intuitively know when you are heading in the right direction. It will feel natural, even when it becomes challenging. From time to time, you can come back to this book—your Journey Map—either to track and appreciate your progress, or to reflect more deeply on areas where the going has been slow.

Your development journey

If you have been working for several years, you have probably already made progress on your development journey. Along the way, you have likely noticed that your development is not a linear process from A to B. You make progress, you have setbacks, and sometimes you feel stuck for a while.

If you know where you are going and have a plan to get there, use this chapter to guide you in refining your next steps. Alternatively, if you need to define a development plan and work on certain things for your vision to become a reality, this chapter will help you move forward on your journey.

EXERCISE: Strategies for your development

Look back at your career to date and think about your education and learning experiences. What were the different options available to you? Which ones helped you progress and which ones did not?

Some typical examples of development options include:

- Professional development: formal training, executive studies, etc.
- Job Experience: daily work, internships, apprenticeships, role changes, etc.
- Personal self-development: books, masterclasses, TED talks, videos online, events, etc.
- Mentoring and coaching: your manager, external resources, professionals, etc.

On the chart below, write down the things that helped you and the things that did not.

EXERCISE: Your development needs

Now that you have reflected on what development options worked in the past, let's examine your situation today. Look closely at the development areas that you have identified earlier in this chapter. Maybe they are related to overcoming a limiting belief, or perhaps they pertain to a specific area where you need to focus in order to achieve one of your aspirations.

Use the chart to capture the areas in which you want to make progress and then match each one with your preferred development option.

My development needs	My development options

Development at work

A key part of your development comes from your work experience: having a good or bad boss; getting a promotion; being made redundant; working on an exciting project. Think about all the things that you are good at today. It is possible, if not probable, that many of them are directly related to your past experiences at work.

Now, let's look to the future.

EXERCISE: Assessing your current work environment

From your work on the previous page, perhaps you have realized that some of your future development needs can be fulfilled in your current work environment.

As you evaluate your development needs, consider how well your current work environment supports your personal and professional growth. Capture your thoughts in the next table.

	What I appreciate about my current work environment	What I am missing in my current work environment
Am I getting better at what I love? **(Passion)**		
Am I getting better at what I do? **(Contribution)**		
Am I allowed to experiment and occasionally fail and grow? **(Psychological Safety)**		
Am I getting feedback on what I am good at and what I need to improve? **(Reward and Recognition)**		
Do I see myself here in the long term? **(Promising Future)**		

Whether or not your current work environment provides you with opportunities to grow, now is the time to make a plan.

EXERCISE: A short-term plan

What would be feasible to accomplish within the next 6–12 months and what needs to happen for you to get there? Write your ideas down. Include things that you can do within your work environment or externally.

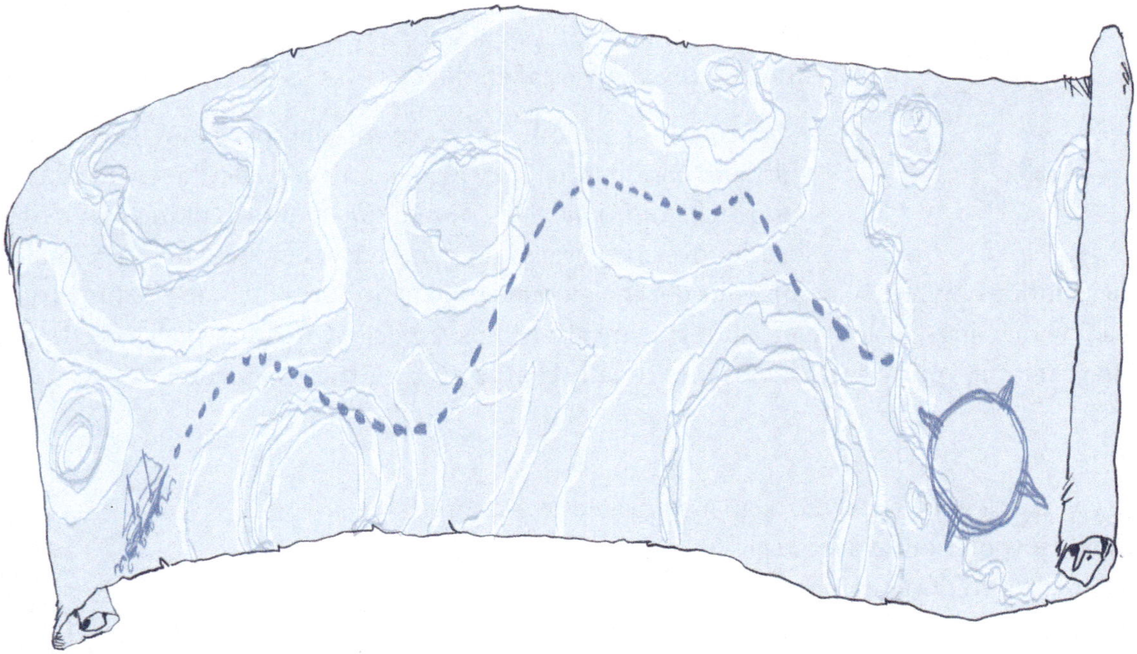

If you feel that your current job no longer supports your development needs, it might be time for a change. This change could be something within your current organization, such as a move to a different department, or it might mean moving to a new organization.

If you are hesitating to make a move, you need to assess why. What is stopping you? Do you need help? You don't have to do it alone.

Development with the help of others

One way to move forward with your development is to get external support by working with a coach or a mentor. This is true whether you are at the beginning of your career or already have several years of experience. To decide whether coaching or mentoring is right for you, you must be clear on what you hope to achieve.

Coaching

You come to a coaching session with a predefined challenge. Examples include: How do I manage stress at the workplace? How do I work with difficult personalities? How do I manage team conflicts or challenging situations? How do I prepare for a management position? How do I influence executive stakeholders?

A coach asks questions and gives you the space to reflect. Coaches create trust and confidence. They help you to consider how you can achieve more and reach your objectives. You do most of the talking. Your coach helps you discover new ways and perspectives on how to tackle challenges. You find most of the solutions by yourself with your coach's guidance. Coaching sessions can be short conversations and limited to a few meetings, or longer-term formal relationships, especially in areas such as getting ready for a promotion or maintaining your position. Coaches usually charge a fee for their services.

Skill mentoring

In this context, you come with a specific challenge related to your job. Examples include: How do I build a strategic plan? How do I assess the risks? How do I create a solution map for a specific area? Skill mentoring is linked to specific tasks that you must do in your daily work.

The mentor usually starts by working with you to reformulate your challenge, helping you see the problem area from different angles. Mentors should be direct about the options that you need to consider, or areas you need to investigate. They should help their mentees ask more questions to go deeper into areas of importance. Together you will figure out a concrete solution for your challenge and develop a plan to do so.

Lifelong mentoring

This type of relationship might begin as a relationship between a manager and a team member, or between a master and an apprentice. It can last for years, decades, or a lifetime, and is characterized by mutual respect, trust, and admiration.

Both parties find value in this relationship. The mentor gets just as much out of it as the mentee. The relationship can start with a simple question or with career guidance. It then evolves into a relationship centered around sharing knowledge, experience, and exploring options to address potential challenges. This type of relationship is less structured than coaching or skill mentoring. It is usually up to the mentee to define the agenda and the value that you wish to receive from this type of relationship.

Due to its less formal and more fluid structure, most mentoring engagements are done for free. This does not mean that the work or commitment on both sides is any less meaningful. Bill Gates, one of the world's most successful businessmen, admits that over the years he has turned to legendary investor Warren Buffet for advice and mentorship on many occasions.

To help decide which, if any, of the above relationships is right for you, ask yourself the following questions:

The most important thing is to find someone whom you trust and respect, and with whom you feel a connection.

Breaking the mold

Elaine is a committed, curious woman with more than five years of professional experience. The purpose of her coaching sessions was to identify her long-term development plan.

Eleven months into the coaching, Elaine had a great opportunity to apply for a job that excited her and for which, she believed, she was a great fit. Did she have years of experience in this type of job? No. Did she have all the required strengths and core capabilities to develop into a great fit for this job? Yes. Did she feel this was the right, motivating, energizing next move for her? Absolutely.

Elaine made it to the final round of interviews, but ultimately did not get the job. During the interviews for the position, she felt that the interviewers were labeling her. They made her feel that she did not fit the mold designed by the company. She was told that in order to get a "similar" kind of job, there is a prescribed career path that she would have to follow, otherwise, those kinds of jobs would not be available to her.

Thanks to the work that Elaine did as part of her coaching sessions, she was able to see beyond that "prescription" which would have sent her in a direction that was not appropriate for her. Elaine felt comfortable with not fitting into a box and with seeing herself for who she truly is. She applied critical thinking to this experience and was able to question, in an objective manner, whether this would have been the right company for her.

Throughout this process, Elaine recognized the benefits of her coaching sessions. She knew that all the work that she had done had been worthwhile. It allowed her to stay confident about her capabilities and strengths. She realized that she did not have to listen to the "advice" she received from her interviewers. After being rejected for the post, Elaine got another job that fit perfectly with her aspirations. She is now fulfilled and happy at work.

1970–2000

2000–2020

2020–...

Ensuring your work environment supports your development

Sometimes you might only stay in a certain workplace for a short period of time. For example, it might soon become clear that the work environment does not align with your values, or that there are limited opportunities for development. Conversely, you might decide to stay in the same environment for many years. Either way, your environment is a key factor to your development, and you should not underestimate its impact on you.

The generations that started work in the 1970s and 1980s were typically able to stay in the same working environment for their whole career. Indeed, it was not unusual for someone to stay in the same job from the first day they started to work. A career path depended heavily on what the workplace offered. There was typically no desire or need to move away from their organization after finishing their studies. People worked in a stable, secure environment.

And then everything changed.

The business world underwent an incredible metamorphosis: global expansion; mergers and acquisitions; outsourcing; the Internet; and more. There were massive transformations as companies grew from national to international, then multinational mega-enterprises.

As a result of these changes, employees began to understand that job security was no longer guaranteed. They started questioning why they were doing what they were doing. Many realized that they should have thought about their personal aspirations and development earlier in order to navigate in such a fluid working environment.

The COVID-19 pandemic shifted workplace change into high gear. Many people were laid off. Many others were forced to work online from home. For at least two years, virtual meetings and working in shorts with kids and pets running around became the norm. It was a stressful situation, but it did give people time to think about their lives, where they were going and whether they were happy with the destination.

The youngest generations are under no illusions about job stability and security. Their only security comes from working on themselves and being confident in their value and impact. They are looking for a place where they can discover and develop their gifts, make a meaningful impactful, and be appreciated.

Today, employees of all generations question why they should stay in a workplace if there is no room for their personal development or if there is no alignment with their aspirations and values.

Taking ownership

Whatever your current situation, you must take ownership for your development path. Thus far in this book, you have explored ways in which to discover your strengths, aspirations, and limiting beliefs. These are the key elements for you to understand your personal requirements, as well as different options you could take on your work-life journey.

You should have a clearer idea of what is important to you, what your development needs are, and why the workplace environment is an essential part of your development.

At the beginning of this chapter, the old English proverb, "Mighty oaks from little acorns grow" was used to illustrate that many elements are required to enable a tree to reach its full potential. This does not imply that a tree must become the tallest or the biggest. Nevertheless, for it to reach its full potential, it must go through many stages of development and growth.

Just as there are no two trees which are the same, your development and growth are unique to you. You cannot simply copy someone else's plan and apply the same strategy or follow the same path.

Your beginnings, your strengths, your experiences, and your decisions all influence your path. Your development happens over time, throughout your work-life journey. There are no shortcuts. It requires strong commitment and consciousness.

Do not wait for someone else to take charge of your development. Think of the opportunity you have in your hands. Consider your potential and how your world would look if you could truly be the best version of yourself.

In the next chapter you will learn how best to apply your unique talents and derive maximum fulfillment and happiness as you continue your development and growth journey.

CHAPTER FIVE

The "Me Magic"

"You can't use up creativity. The more you use, the more you have."
– Maya Angelou

What makes you so special?

We all have it when we are born: the desire to explore and discover. A desire that leads to creativity and innovation. When we create, there is an innate sense of satisfaction and achievement. This satisfaction comes from something unique that you have done. It could be as simple as building a sandcastle on the beach or as complex as the coding for the latest app that everyone is using. This uniqueness is the essence of what we call the "Me Magic."

As we grow older, this sense of satisfaction might come from the planning and creation of a meal or some special moment for someone dear to you. There might be an activity in your life in which you are able to express your creativity through art and design, music, or a myriad of other activities. Maybe you still enjoy making sandcastles on the beach.

This feeling of creative satisfaction is special. It is empowering; it is unique to you. Your purpose in doing these things might be driven by a desire for personal satisfaction or some benefit that you are giving to others.

When we innovate, we come up with new ideas, often to solve a problem. To do this, we combine our skills with our creativity to generate ideas that lead to solutions.

Those skilled at innovation are able to move beyond the obvious and come up with breakthrough ideas that have a "wow" factor. Once seen, it is hard to imagine how we could have lived without that innovative idea or invention. Indeed, the best innovations are often the most obvious after we have seen them.

Take a moment to think about the wonders of the World Wide Web and the Internet. If they seem ordinary and do not fill you with a feeling of awe, try to imagine the world without them. Later in this chapter, we will take a closer look at the English innovator Sir Tim Berners-Lee, inventor of the World Wide Web, to explore what motivates this iconic, creative innovator to continue to pioneer and develop new ideas. We will also look at others who built on those ideas to create further breakthroughs.

Releasing your magic at work

Do you have that same feeling of creative satisfaction with your work? Are you using your "Me Magic" at work? Are you motivated to explore and discover, to apply your creativity and innovate, to come up with new ideas, and to find ways of doing things better?

If so, fantastic! This chapter will help you enhance your creativity and apply your innovation at work so that you can help others achieve the same level of satisfaction. It will motivate you to take your creativity and innovation to another level.

If you are not motivated, do not despair. Many studies show that only a minority of respondents feel that they are living up to their creative potential. These studies confirm a comment frequently attributed to Pablo Picasso: All children are born artists, the problem is how to remain an artist as we grow up.

Fortunately, creativity is something innate to humans, and it can be rekindled.

In this chapter, you will discover how to bring creativity and innovation into your daily work life and how to ignite your "Me Magic." You might even find that this discovery extends beyond your daily work and can be applied to other aspects of your life. Such an outcome would be ideal, and it is something for which you should strive.

When you get the creativity and innovation formula right, you will have a strong desire to improve your attitude and your contributions to the work that you do. You will increase the satisfaction that you derive from working with your colleagues. You will get that buzz, that spark of enthusiasm to ignite your new ideas and to see those ideas make a positive impact on your organization.

As your confidence grows from this renewed approach to work, it will have a transformative impact not just on you, but on your colleagues and your organization. In turn, this will change the nature of your work and the creative satisfaction you derive from it, which will lead to further transformation opportunities. It is a virtuous circle.

But first, we must dig deeper to understand why your creativity and innovation are critical to your personal journey, your career, and the value that you can contribute. It is equally important to understand why your company needs to value your engagement and personal development in this way.

Sorry, Rolling Stones, you can get satisfaction

Developing a deeper understanding of why creativity is important for you is both rewarding and fun. It also demands a serious commitment from you. A commitment to take your creative ideas forward and make things happen. It will become an important tenet of your life and a hallmark of the contributions that you make to the organizations in which you work.

At the most fundamental level, the importance of creativity is the feeling of satisfaction that it brings to you. The word "satisfaction" itself carries with it many personal interpretations.

The seminal work and research of the Hungarian-American psychologist Mihaly Csikszentmihalyi used the concept of "flow" to refer to a state of optimal experience. This is a particular aspect of satisfaction that you can experience. When in this state of flow, you focus in such a way that you lose yourself and your sense of time and you concentrate solely on whatever you are doing. Nothing else matters.

Anyone can enter a state of flow: a composer deeply immersed in the creative process of writing a piece of music; a computer programmer designing a new algorithm to solve a complex problem; a mountain climber about to reach the summit of a difficult climb. This feeling can also be experienced with simple everyday activities like gardening, completing a crossword puzzle, or building a model airplane.

The concept of flow has been explored in Eastern and Western cultures and civilizations over millennia. In Japanese Zen Buddhism, *mushin no shin* refers to a state of awareness that means "mind of no mind," where thoughts and emotions do not get in the way of achieving peak performance. It is a central concept in Japanese martial arts. Likewise, in Chinese philosophy, *wu wei* refers to the notion of effortless action or effortless doing. More specifically, it means being at peace while engaged in a task so that you can carry out the task with maximum skill and efficiency.

We have a good understanding of how biology helps us to experience a state of flow. In Chapter 3 we spoke about the neurotransmitters that spark chemical messages to release hormones. When these hormones are released, they impact performance. We know that serotonin creates the "feel good" factor. In addition, norepinephrine and dopamine help improve focus and block out distractions. Endorphins relieve stress and help block out pain.

Everyone can experience the state of flow in different contexts, no matter how significant or insignificant the activity might seem. Can you remember a time when you were so completely absorbed in doing something that you were impervious to what was happening around you? And, when you finally looked at your watch, you could not believe how quickly the time had passed?

We just have to recognize and be aware of the conditions that are necessary to get into that flow state.

EXERCISE: When do you experience flow?

Above, write down examples of times when you have experienced a state of flow. Think about the conditions that allowed you to enter that state. What were you doing? Where were you doing it? With whom were you doing it?

The experiences could be simple (going for a walk in the forest; completing a jigsaw puzzle) or complex (learning a new skill on an online platform; finishing an important project for a client).

The size of the bubbles above represent the relative feeling of flow that you experienced. The bigger the bubble, the deeper the state of flow.

There is a close association between creativity and the concept of flow. When you are truly engaged in a creative activity, you enter a state of flow. This association underpins important factors that lead to personal growth and satisfaction. This feeling of flow provides the motivation to master skills and apply them to rewarding, meaningful challenges. If you care about your personal growth and tap into your creativity, a unique and enriching kind of personal fulfillment can open up for you.

In the zone

In the previous chapter, you looked at your strengths and skills. Now think about a time when you successfully used those strengths or skills. Were you totally engaged and present when you were involved in this activity? Did you have a feeling of satisfaction during or after the event? If so, there is a good chance that you were in the flow channel. Many people refer to it as being "in the zone". The flow channel is the zone in which an activity challenges your skills in a stimulating and rewarding way.

Of course, there are times when you will be outside your flow channel. If you are highly skilled at something but the challenge is not great enough, there is a good chance that you will be bored. Conversely, if the challenge is too great for your skill level, you will likely feel frustrated. It is important to be aware of these boundaries to your flow channel.

In Chapter 3, we discussed extrinsic rewards or accolades that provide recognition of your achievements. These are important external signs of success. But the intrinsic feeling of satisfaction that you derive from applying or using your skills is a reward that is unique to you. The feeling of satisfaction that you experience during and after your accomplishment cannot be taken away from you.

If you understand this feeling and can tap into it, it can become addictive in a good way. It can be the motivation to develop and master your skills further, to apply those skills to greater challenges, and to experience a more intense state of flow from a wider range of things that you do.

Entering the flow channel

The "feel-good" factor is powerful because it allows you to tap into your "Me Magic." But it is not just about you; it is also about what you can contribute to others.

When you have a deeper understanding of yourself and what makes you tick, everything around you changes in a positive way. You begin to see situations and opportunities differently. You have a greater understanding of your unique talents and how you can use them to help others.

When you think about your work, there will be things that you love, things that you tolerate, and things that you dislike. You were able to explore some of these things in Chapters 2 and 3. Each of them contains opportunities for creativity. Each experience—positive or negative—can provide opportunities for you to think differently about why you are doing an activity, how you are doing it, and what you hope to achieve.

If you take time to reflect on these aspects of your work, you can see what level of satisfaction you derive from each. You can identify opportunities to amplify the positive aspects. You can apply your creativity and innovation to change your approach regarding areas of work that you consider to be less than perfect.

This introspection into your personal satisfaction and approach to creating space for entering your flow channel does not depend on others. Being content and simply deriving satisfaction from the way you do things is a sufficient reward. However, the greatest benefits come from sharing your insights with others.

Black belt

In martial arts such as judo or karate, progress through the various stages of learning is recognized by the color of the belt that they are allowed to wear when in the dojo. Each belt—yellow, orange, green, blue, brown, black—represents a level of achievement. For many, the ultimate achievement is the coveted black belt.

The reason for speaking about this method of grading is twofold. First, there is a sense of achievement and satisfaction when successfully being awarded the next grade and belt. Second, the grading system helps you to master certain techniques at each stage to improve your skills.

However, in martial arts, being awarded a black belt is not the end of the journey; in fact, it is just the beginning. Developing beyond what is known as a first dan grade (black belt), requires you to contribute back to the martial art itself. Teaching is part of this journey to pass on your knowledge to others.

Moving beyond what you have learned, to create and innovate, requires additional insight to become a true master. Your initial training and development provide a foundation that allows you to innovate.

This analogy can be applied directly to your working life. You may not be awarded colored belts in the workplace, but by developing your skills and expertise in your chosen field, you are creating a foundation upon which you can innovate. Your qualifications and experience are the starting point for you to be able to find your voice and make your personal contribution. This concept is explored in detail by Stephen R. Covey in his book *The 8th Habit: From Effectiveness to Greatness*.

Why flow at work is important

So far, we have only been speaking about your personal feeling of satisfaction from the work that you do and its relationship to your skills, your challenges, and the feeling of flow that you can experience. By mastering your skills and expertise, you are more able to focus your creativity and innovate to reach higher levels of satisfaction from your work. And these benefits can extend to your company, provided that the company is prepared to do its part.

When a workplace has the right conditions to allow people to enter their flow channel, the potential is enormous. People are motivated to do their best in their respective fields of expertise and responsibility. Ideas abound and flourish. But are companies alone responsible for creating these conditions?

It is easy to point fingers and say that it is the responsibility of management. You might also have a management responsibility. If so, finger-pointing will not help. You are also responsible for making this happen. In the same way that we have just explored personal satisfaction for you as an individual, employees in a healthy company should also be able to collectively feel satisfied and proud of their achievements.

Does this always happen though? How many companies have become well established and then started to stagnate? Even some of the iconic greats such as Apple are targets for this criticism. They often struggle for innovation and breakthrough insights for what to do next. Employees can also feel disconnected within fast-paced companies when their personal contributions get lost amongst the noise of the apparent rapid progress and change.

Instead of a vibrant culture of employee engagement, there can be a culture of pressure, apathy, and disempowerment. An employee approach of "wait and see" can creep in. Knowing that change will come, it is easy to allow apathy and anticipation to dramatically reduce the level of engagement.

Contrary to experiencing a desired state of being motivated by the work that they do and the contributions that they make, many seek alternative outlets for their satisfaction. They might place an increased emphasis on the importance of outside interests, vacations, or in the worst case, coming up with creative ideas on how to take sick leave. As mentioned earlier, this phenomenon has come to be known as "quiet quitting."

Your workplace has a major influence on your ability to enter your flow channel. A stimulating environment of creativity and innovation can help you steer into your flow channel and stay there. A negative, demotivating environment can just as easily knock you out of it.

Lessons from Gore (Bill, not Al)

It is interesting to learn from the insights developed by Bill Gore, the founder of W. L. Gore & Associates, Inc. He had a fundamental belief in the individual and adopted a guiding principle of freedom in the way he developed the company. Gore's approach created a lattice-style organization in which every individual is connected to every other.

The goal was to eliminate layers of management so that information would flow in every direction. Individuals and self-managed teams could go to anyone to get what they needed to be successful. There is a famous story about a new employee who went and introduced himself to Bill Gore on his first day. He asked Gore what he should do and Gore responded that he should go have a look around and find something in which he was interested. The new employee did and that began a long career in the company.

As the organization grew to over 9,000 employees, a key learning was that facilities should not grow above approximately 250 employees to maintain this level of autonomy and innate drive. Gore also believed that if employees were passionate about their work, they would naturally be highly self-motivated. Having smaller business unit facilities created a context that helped maintain this passion.

Even the selection of W. L. Gore & Associates, Inc.'s CEO is a peer-driven selection process. Terri Kelly, who served as President and CEO from 2005–2018, joined Gore as a process engineer in 1983.

Clearly, it is not just the number of people that matters. The point is that creativity and innovation within a company thrive on collaboration. Your own personal skills in creativity and innovation will also benefit from a company culture where collaboration is supported and encouraged.

Alone and together

This discussion of creativity and flow raises an important question: is it better to work alone or together? Does your feeling of satisfaction in the flow channel reach its maximum when you are left alone to focus, or do you thrive when interacting with other colleagues?

There are different factors to consider when answering this question. Your personality has an impact on how you like to work. However, it is not "all or nothing." There are times when working alone is preferable and times when collaboration is better. From a creativity and innovation perspective, some important observations can be made.

Apocryphally, when the Greek polymath Archimedes stepped into a full bathtub and the water overflowed, he exclaimed, "Eureka!" (I have found it!). Archimedes had discovered a way to determine the mass of an object by the quantity of water that it displaced. In life, however, true Eureka moments are rare.

There are certainly times when you will have a flash of inspiration on your own. These are the moments when you suddenly have a breakthrough in solving a problem. However, when we read about famous Eureka moments, we imagine magical events of creativity and innovation. The reality is that moments such as these are often a culmination of many other individual and collective experiences.

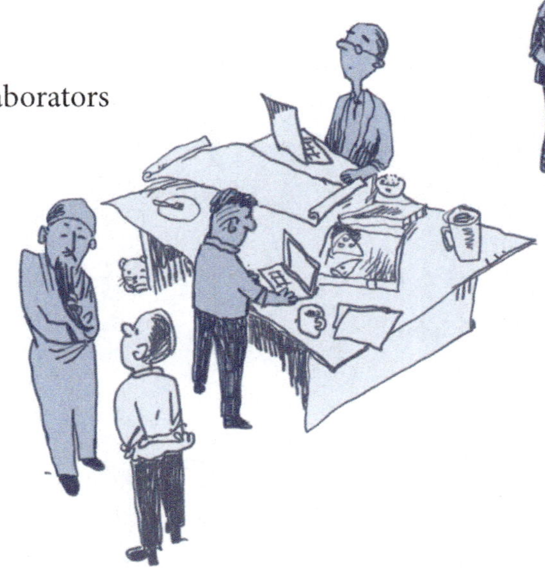

For example, Tim Berners-Lee, had many collaborators while working at CERN, the European Particle Physics Laboratory located near Geneva, Switzerland. Berners-Lee acknowledges that his personal approach to creativity, invention, and innovation has depended on many years of collaboration and collective thinking with others. That said, he enjoys his solitude and prefers to work alone. He needs time to contemplate his ideas without interruption. This approach enables him to be highly creative to develop insights to solve practical problems.

Singer-songwriter Amanda Palmer often speaks about how creativity and innovation are all about collecting and connecting "dots," and then sharing them with others. By "dots" she means the observations and insights and experiences that we all accumulate as we go through life. Palmer explores these, and other useful, ideas in her book, *The Art of Asking: or How I Learned to Stop Worrying and Let People Help*.

Do you thrive on your own or with the stimulation of working with others? Being self-aware in this respect can help you seek out moments of isolation or interaction that fuel your creativity. Whichever you prefer, you will most probably have to spend time doing both. Go back to page 148 where you listed examples of times when you have entered the flow channel. Were you alone or with others? Perhaps you have examples of each.

Whether you prefer to work alone or with others, you will have the greatest impact if you learn how to enter the flow channel in any situation.

What difference does it make?

Depending on your role in your organization, you might think that your personal "Me Magic" is not relevant to the job that you do. The qualifications and skills that you have should be aligned to the position and terms of reference for your job. You have clearly defined objectives; you know how to achieve those objectives and you are rewarded and compensated based on your ability to do your job. Why rock the boat? If you just do your job, you can progress in your career, support your family, have time to pursue hobbies, and work toward a happy retirement.

But what if something changes? What happens then? How resilient are you to adapt to change? How resilient is your organization to adapt to changes when the business climate changes? Conversely, what if nothing changes? How happy are you with the status quo? Is there a danger of personal stagnation?

It is time to explore how your ideas can be made to matter, how they can make a difference not only to the success of your company, but more importantly to the satisfaction that you derive from the work that you do.

What if?

Have you ever been standing in a long queue at the check-out lane of a supermarket and thought, what if they opened more check-out lanes at peak times like this? What if they had a better system to plan when they needed more staff? What if I had known there was going to be this delay and could have come at a different time? If any of these questions have crossed your mind, congratulations! You have just engaged in "what if" reasoning.

Questioning the current situation is a great starting point for developing your own innovative ideas. If your queueing time is long enough, you might also start innovating ahead of the need. Why do we need a check-out at all? Could there be a better system?

Fortunately, many fellow queuers in the past have done this and they have also developed their ideas further. For example, many locations now have self-scanning, self-service check-out options, even automated trolley scans. Amazon and Whole Foods now have stores that detect when you enter via an app on your phone. You take whatever you want off the shelf, put it in your bag and walk out. The system knows exactly what you have taken, and the relevant amount is deducted from your e-wallet.

Does your "what if" thinking stop when you see these innovations being implemented? We hope not, because there will always be another problem to solve. When you purchase alcohol, how does the store verify that you are the legal age? Is there a need for the flashing red lights to attract the attention of a supervisor? What if they knew who you were as a frequent customer? What if there were a better way?

The journey of observation, curiosity, and "what if" thinking should be continuous in every aspect of life, even supermarket shopping.

Questioning the status quo and innovating ahead of the need is something that we can all do. It is fun and opens a new dimension of curiosity and observation about the things we do, what others do, and how things can be improved.

EXERCISE: What if?

Try a "what if" thinking exercise now. Grab a pen and paper and brainstorm five ideas to solve each of the issues below. That's twenty-five ideas in total. The key to this exercise is not to self-edit as you do it. Don't cross ideas out or second guess yourself. Just write down whatever comes to mind no matter how ridiculous it might seem.

- Reducing your commute time to work
- Avoiding running out of coffee or tea
- Fake news
- Climate change
- Any problem that bothers you

What did you come up with? How did you find the process? Were you tempted to dwell on any of your ideas and start thinking about the challenges to implement them?

When engaging in "what if" thinking, it is important to let the ideas flow. Always fill your idea quota, such as five ideas for each of the topics in the exercise above. Often the first few ideas are the obvious ones. Then, as you start to dig deeper, the more radical, breakthrough ideas start to reveal themselves.

Do not worry if you do not come up with lots of ideas quickly. Take a break and come back to the list later. Or go for a walk and take your list with you. Ideas can strike at the most unexpected times, especially when you are not focusing on the subject.

From the supermarket to the office

If standing in line at the supermarket checkout is painful, consider your experience with business meetings. How often have you sat in a meeting and thought: What if there were a clear agenda for this meeting? What if I could share my ideas with this group?

Have you ever attended a meeting where afterwards you thought that it was a complete waste of time? Perhaps it was poorly organized; perhaps it had no relevance for your work; perhaps people strayed from the agenda and nothing was decided. We certainly have been in meetings like that. How could you bring "what if" thinking to this situation?

Why not call a meeting about how to run efficient meetings? Send out an agenda beforehand. Tell people to come with three concrete ideas. Start and end your meeting at the scheduled times. Assign responsibility for any follow-up work.

Of course, there have to be limits to how far you can take this heightened approach to your personal creativity and innovation. It would quickly become exhausting to constantly be looking for ways to solve the problems that you observe in daily life.

However, developing these skills is an important part of exploring your full potential as an innovator. In turn, this will have a positive impact on your ability to mature, master your personal skills, and enhance the satisfaction that you derive from applying those skills. This is how you develop the "Me Magic."

One thing to keep in mind when exploring and expanding your "what if" thinking is your personal perspective. We all have one. Depending on your personality, role, education, and experience, you will see the world in a certain way. For example, your perspective as a shopper in a supermarket is different from that of a store manager or cashier.

Right on track

A few years ago, ideas were being developed to make advances with the Eurostar train service. The engineering mindset was keen to reduce travel time by improving the tracks. Eventually, the travel time between London and Paris was reduced by forty minutes, but at a cost of six billion Euros.

A more passenger-focused mindset might have been first to spend a fraction of this amount by adding Wi-Fi to improve the travel experience. In fact, some travelers actually appreciated the journey more when the trip was longer.

Keeping this example in mind, you can see that it is important to explore “what if” scenarios from different points of view. These are often called personas; you put yourself conceptually in the shoes of another persona when exploring your own ideas.

EXERCISE: Perspectives on a problem

Think of an issue in your company that you would like to see changed or resolved. It can be anything and does not necessarily have to be related to work-related matters.

Issue: ____

How might different people try to resolve the issue? Try to put yourself in the shoes of others in addition to coming up with your own ideas.

CEO Manager Secretary Client Sales Department Marketing Department Other

Breaking down barriers

Letting your ideas flow freely is an essential part of "what if" thinking. But it is not sufficient. Equally important is the ability to identify potential barriers. They either slow you down or prevent you from achieving an objective. You started to explore examples of barriers in the previous chapter when looking at your limiting beliefs that might prevent you from achieving your aspirations.

Let's return to that annoying supermarket queue. (It hasn't moved much.) Having thought about some of the "what if" solutions, what sorts of barriers can you imagine that will make those solutions difficult to achieve? In other words, what are the possible reasons why the managers of the supermarket company have not already done something to improve the check-out customer experience. After all, they can see the lines. They must know what is happening in their stores.

Is it a question of employee costs? Is there a lack of planning data to estimate peak shopping times? Or is something more intentional happening? Maybe the supermarket wants you to wait. Studies have shown that when people wait in line, they (and their children) will use that time to look at the items on the shelves by the cash desks—magazines, chewing gum, candies, etc. A lot of spontaneous shopping is done at the cash desk and that helps the bottom line of the supermarket.

By taking time to think about potential barriers to your ideas, you have probably also moved to the front of the queue! Perhaps more importantly, you have also taken the next important step to develop your innovative thinking.

Just because you identify barriers to your idea, it does not mean that your idea has no merit. In the previous chapter you were encouraged to identify your limiting beliefs. These are the beliefs that can prevent you from achieving your aspirations. They are barriers that should become additional focus areas for your "what if" thinking skills. Barriers themselves can become mini projects. If you can remove or minimize the impact of a potential barrier, then progress towards achieving success to implement your big idea or achieve your aspiration suddenly becomes a lot easier.

If you find yourself struggling to overcome a barrier—as will inevitably happen from time to time when working on a worthwhile project—go easy on yourself. Take a break. For a couple of hours or perhaps a couple of days. Let the problem sit and work on something unrelated. It will give your active mind a rest while the subconscious continues to process ideas. Think of it as sending your brain to a spa. Then, when you return to the problem, you might see it in a different light and solutions that had previously gone unnoticed will reveal themselves.

We take a closer look at barriers in Chapter 8.

A little less conversation, a little more action

With practice, engaging in "what if" thinking should become second nature. As you develop insights into the ways that creativity and innovation can play a role in your daily life, your working life, and the life of your organization, a new world of opportunities opens up.

However, taking the time to engage in "what if" thinking is the easy part. If you do not do something with your ideas, the time that you have taken to explore these possibilities will have been for nought. You have to make things happen.

Taking action is the most difficult part of developing your creative ideas. Your ideas, observations, and insights will come more easily as you practice being aware of what is happening around you. But deciding to do something with your ideas can be a challenge. That itself is another barrier. And this barrier is constantly being reinforced by a small, powerful word: "but."

How often have you come across a situation that needs to be changed and you say to yourself, "Yes, but …."

"Yes, but ...

What if you substituted the word "and" for "but"? It can influence your thinking process to find solutions. For example, imagine that on your first day of vacation, it is pouring rain. If you say, "I'm on vacation, but it's raining" you are thinking of the rain as a problem or barrier. However, if you say, "I'm on vacation and it's raining" it opens up a different line of inquiry: "So now I can read the novel that I've wanted to read" or "now I can take that cooking class."

The same holds true for work: "Yes, it's a good idea and we don't have the money. So, we can start budgeting now to implement the idea next year, or we can take out a loan to follow through now because the profits will more than offset the cost."

Get your priorities straight

There needs to be some way to prioritize and select the ideas and opportunities that really matter. The first filter can simply be to ask yourself: Will this idea add value? Will it make a difference? You can usually find ways to convince yourself that your idea could make a difference and that it is the right thing to do. However, you need to develop a comprehensive way to think through the filtering process.

When you have decided to focus on a particular initiative, gathering and receiving feedback on your idea is essential. You might feel the need to keep it to yourself for fear of ridicule, or perhaps you do not want somebody else to steal it. However, being open and sharing your ideas is necessary and yields many benefits.

You will develop new insights to refine and improve your idea by speaking with others. There may be possibilities to combine your idea with the ideas of others to have an even greater impact.

There is an old adage that says if I have an apple and you have an apple, and I give you my apple you give me yours, we still each have one apple. But if I have an idea, and you have an idea, and I give you my idea and you give me yours, now we each have two ideas.

As momentum builds, the enthusiasm that grows around your idea will provide you with more motivation to take things further. You will start to have a clearer idea of what can be done and the unique value that you might be able to contribute.

Ideas come and go. The art of identifying, exploring, and developing your ideas is in itself an important exercise for your personal mastery of creativity and innovation. However, making things happen is where the real satisfaction starts.

What do I need to do to get started?

There are some simple steps that you can take to pay more attention to your creative and innovative contributions in your work. There are ways to develop your skills as an innovator as well as tools that can help you to identify creative new ideas that add value to the work that you do and the contributions to your company.

We would like to offer a simple framework to help you to structure your approach to innovation. We will introduce tools and exercises to help you focus on specific problems. But this is only the starting point. As soon as you start to reap the benefits and feel the satisfaction from developing your own innovation agenda, your journey will really begin to flow. You will continue exploring and discovering new ways to master creativity and innovation in all aspects of your life.

Take a stab at it

Getting started with a new initiative can be a challenge. Facing a blank sheet of paper can be daunting. You can easily get distracted, perhaps making a cup of tea or coffee, checking social media, and so on.

We believe that there are four elements that can help you jumpstart your creativity and innovation. They are captured in the acronym "STAB."

Space

You need a suitable space in which to work. Do you have a place where you can do creativework? It could be a physical space at work, a room in your house, or somewhere else. If not, can you make one, either where you live or in some other location? The key is that you put yourself in a ready state so that you can focus on your thoughts and creativity.

Time

You need to take the time to be in that space so that you can work on your ideas. Look at your calendar for the coming two weeks. Can you block off some time every day for creative thinking and work? You can start with small blocks of time of thirty minutes or less, but consistency is key. And, if these blocks of time can be at the same time every day, it will strengthen the creativity habit.

Action

Once you come up with an idea that you want to develop, what action will you take? You need to do something with your idea. Will you seek help from others? Will you share your idea? Will you invest time, energy, or money to bring it to life? If you do not act, it is almost a waste of time to have had the idea in the first place.

Belief

Believing in your ideas is critical. Even if your first drafts are less than perfect (which they most likely will be) by taking the time to work on your ideas, you will improve them. This, in turn, strengthens your belief in them. When acting on your idea you run into obstacles, but your belief will help you adapt and find solutions.

Your creative energy

In addition to the above elements, you have to pay attention to your personal creative energy. It goes beyond thinking about your own talents and skills as a creative innovator and relates to the inner spark that allows your capabilities to flourish.

The factors that influence your energy level are unique to you. These factors might include diet, exercise, music, reading, or meditation. One essential factor that is also one of the most overlooked in terms of your creative energy, is sleep.

In his bestselling book, *Why We Sleep: Unlocking the Power of Sleep and Dreams*, Matthew Walker sets out the extensive and compelling research on sleep and why we should take it more seriously. He gives practical advice on how to improve the quality of your sleep so that you get the maximum benefit from it. These tips, espoused by other experts, include keeping the room where you sleep cool, reducing the amount of blue light (from computers and cell phones) in the hour before you sleep, and what to do if you cannot fall asleep immediately.

EXERCISE: Energy boosters

It is up to you to determine the elements that spark your creativity. Write down three things or activities that always give you a burst of creative energy.

1. ____

2. ____

3. ____

If you are serious about being creative, you need to be serious about those factors in your life that both enhance your creativity or diminish it.

Fire away

In his book *Beyond the Obvious: Killer Questions that Spark Game-Changing Innovation*, American businessman Phil McKinney introduces a simple framework that will help get you started identifying your breakthrough ideas. It is based on the acronym "FIRE": Focus, Ideate, Rank, and Execute.

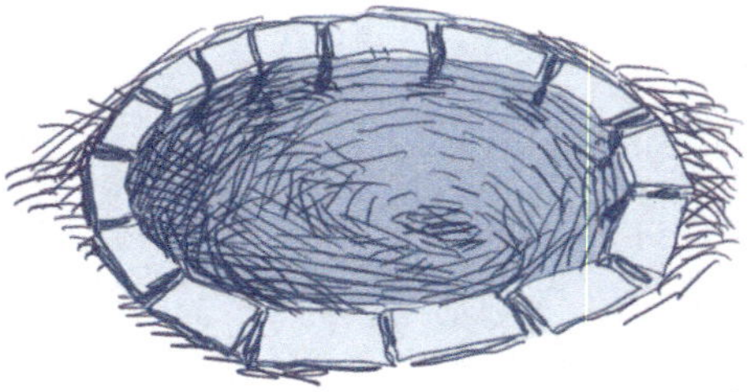

Focus

Focusing on the innovation search involves taking the time to map out all of the areas of interest. Let's return to the frustration of being in that supermarket checkout queue again. If you take a few moments to think about the problem, how many different areas can you think about that might be worthy of some attention?

The scheduling of checkout operators is just one topic. How about the design of the store layout to provide sufficient room to queue? What sort of experience is being created in that queuing time? Are there benefits associated with spending time in the queue? Could there be a reward if your queuing time is greater than a certain limit? If you are a frequent loyal customer, should you be entitled to join a special check-out lane? What products should be on display to make the waiting time worthwhile?

Each of the identified topics could be worth exploring further. To begin with, take time to fully explore the different areas to consider. You can then take each area in turn to apply your creative thinking. Do not try to cover all of the areas at once. Depth is better than breadth, and each area deserves full exploration.

In his work in research and experience as an innovator, Danish author Thomas Wedell-Wedellsborg devoted particular attention to focusing on the right things. He asks the question, "What's your problem?" and advocates that to solve the toughest problems you should consider first changing the problems that you solve. In other words, take the time to fully understand and define the problem before you start exploring solutions.

Wedell-Wedellsborg explores the classic elevator problem. Similar to the challenges of supermarket queues, he reveals some interesting insights into dealing with the challenges of providing a rewarding elevator experience in a tall building. Have you ever wondered why many elevators have a mirror inside of them? Does this help you to enjoy your journey and temporarily forget about the time that you spent waiting for the elevator to arrive?

Behavioral science shows that installing a mirror (and/or video, poster, etc.) can have a positive impact on your elevator experience. These things can compensate for any frustration that you might experience while waiting for the elevator to arrive. As with the Eurostar example on page 162, by reframing the problem—is it one of speed, or rather about creating a better travel experience—it is often possible to discover breakthroughs and innovative solutions.

Ideate

Ideation is all about coming up with new ideas and then exploring them further. Some of your ideas might seem obvious and you might wonder why somebody else has not already thought of them. On the other end of the spectrum, you might come up with ideas that seem completely crazy.

At this stage, do not reject an idea because it is obvious or crazy (or anything in between). Capture them all. Keep generating ideas. Do not question, criticize, or discard your ideas. Allow your mind to roam freely and explore.

Here is a fun exercise that can help with ideation. Find two or three common household items: a spoon, fork, toothpick, elastic band, ball, etc. Anything will do. Now, pick one of the items and set a timer for one minute. In that time, write down as many creative uses for the object as you can, even if they have nothing to do with the way in which it is normally used.

For example, if you chose toothpicks, your list might include:

- Toothpicks
- Kindling for a small fire
- Miniature chopsticks
- Miniature pool cues

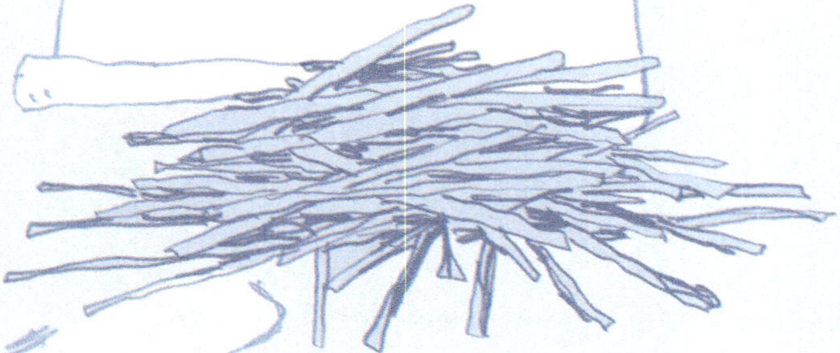

Repeat the process with a second household item, say, a dish.

- Dish
- Frisbee
- Tiny shield
- Heavy handheld fan

Now, for the third round, come up with ideas that involve combining the previous two items, in this case, a toothpick and a dish. (If you do not immediately understand the ideas below, think about them for a while.)

- Clock
- Difficult plate-spinning act
- Shelter for bugs
- Sundial

Rank

Ranking your ideas requires a disciplined evaluation of their feasibility. There are a number of factors to consider, the most important of which is the value that the idea could deliver and the people who would benefit. As you explored in the exercise on page 163, considering different personas is important when trying to rank ideas.

Once you have chosen the ideas, for each one you then need to consider other factors, including:

- Can you get people excited about your idea?
- Do you have the skills to do something with your idea?
- How expensive will it be to carry out the idea?
- Can you get assistance—financial or technical—from your company or elsewhere?
- What is the first step that you can take to build momentum?

Depending on how you answer these questions (and others that you might have), you can reorder your ideas in terms of which ones you will tackle first. That leads us to the final and most important step in the process.

Execute

It is only by taking action that your creative and innovative insights will have any impact on the world. What good is it if your ideas remain scribbled notes on paper or ephemeral thoughts in your head? You must act.

It begins with a first step. Psychologists have found that when people take even a small first step, the chances that they will go further are greatly increased. Each successive step increases the momentum that will ultimately lead to completion.

So, think big but start small. In recent times, the concept of "minimum viable solutions" has become the terminology of choice. Other maxims like "Fail early, fail fast" can help remind you that the journey will not always be smooth. To the contrary, you will encounter challenges, setbacks, and disappointments along the way. They are all part of the process.

You need to set realistic expectations and constantly assess your progress, and when necessary, make the appropriate adjustments. All of this will require resilience on your part to keep going. Accept that the journey will not always be easy and be kind to yourself when things do not go as planned. Take time to eat properly, exercise, and get sufficient rest. Revisit the ideas that you noted on page 171 that give you creative energy and draw on them regularly.

Finally, as you advance with your creative and innovative ideas, don't forget to celebrate your successes. Be proud of your achievements and enjoy the moment.

Next on the agenda

By doing the exercises in this chapter, you have already made a good start. You have taken the time to explore your ideas and be creative. It was time well spent. The next step will be to apply this same approach to your work and your personal life. A good approach will be for you to develop the habit of writing down your ideas. In this regard, we recommend that you get two notebooks.

The first is your Innovation Agenda. In this document, you write down all the things that you want to address and your ideas for doing so. It should be a living document, "not a static to-do list. Your Innovation Agenda is your personal priority list that you can use to guide and focus your creativity and innovation.

The second document is your Idea Book. When you have a good idea, write it down. When you have a bad idea, write it down. When you see something interesting, write it down. When you have a question … you get the idea. With your Idea Book, you are "collecting dots" that might not seem relevant now, but which could be important in the future. The concept of an Idea Book is not new.

The historical legacy of Charles Darwin is well known. Less well known is the fact that his grandfather, Erasmus Darwin, kept an "Idea Book," which in those days, was known as a "Commonplace Book." Erasmus was a respected physician and a well-known poet, philosopher, botanist, and naturalist. As a botanist he formulated one of the first formal theories of evolution, the Laws of Organic Life.

Erasmus made many entries in his Commonplace Book. It was typical practice in the Renaissance period and in the nineteenth century. However you like to capture ideas, give it a try. Your next great idea is just a thought away.

By keeping your own Idea Book, you will be able to identify ways to improve and master your skills. This personal growth will enhance the satisfaction that you will receive from using your skills to tackle bigger challenges. As the Russian composer and pianist Dimitri Shostakovich said, "A creative artist works on his next composition because he was not satisfied with his previous one."

Improving through improv

Another great way to explore your "Me Magic" further is to enter the world of theatrical improvisation, typically referred to as "improv." Improv has been shown to be effective to help boost creativity, confidence, and overall mental health. It forces you to go outside of your typical comfort zone.

In the world of improv, you have players (actors) on stage who get suggestions from the audience about things such as a location, relationship, object, or situation. The players must then create a scene on the spot without any preparation. Characters, dialogue, and plot are all invented in the moment. Improv is fast, fun, and unpredictable. People end up exploring ideas they were not even thinking of just moments earlier, and the results are spontaneous and often hilarious. Yet there is a serious side to improv.

Improv teaches skills such as quick thinking, cooperation, active listening, creativity, and leadership. When these skills are applied in business, great things can happen; it's no longer "business as usual."

Studies have shown that regular improv classes enable participants to be more creative, think in more diverse ways, and break away from fixed patterns of behavior. Self-esteem and confidence improve, and participants are able to accept other people's ideas and add to them.

We will have more to say about improv later.

PART THREE

FLOW

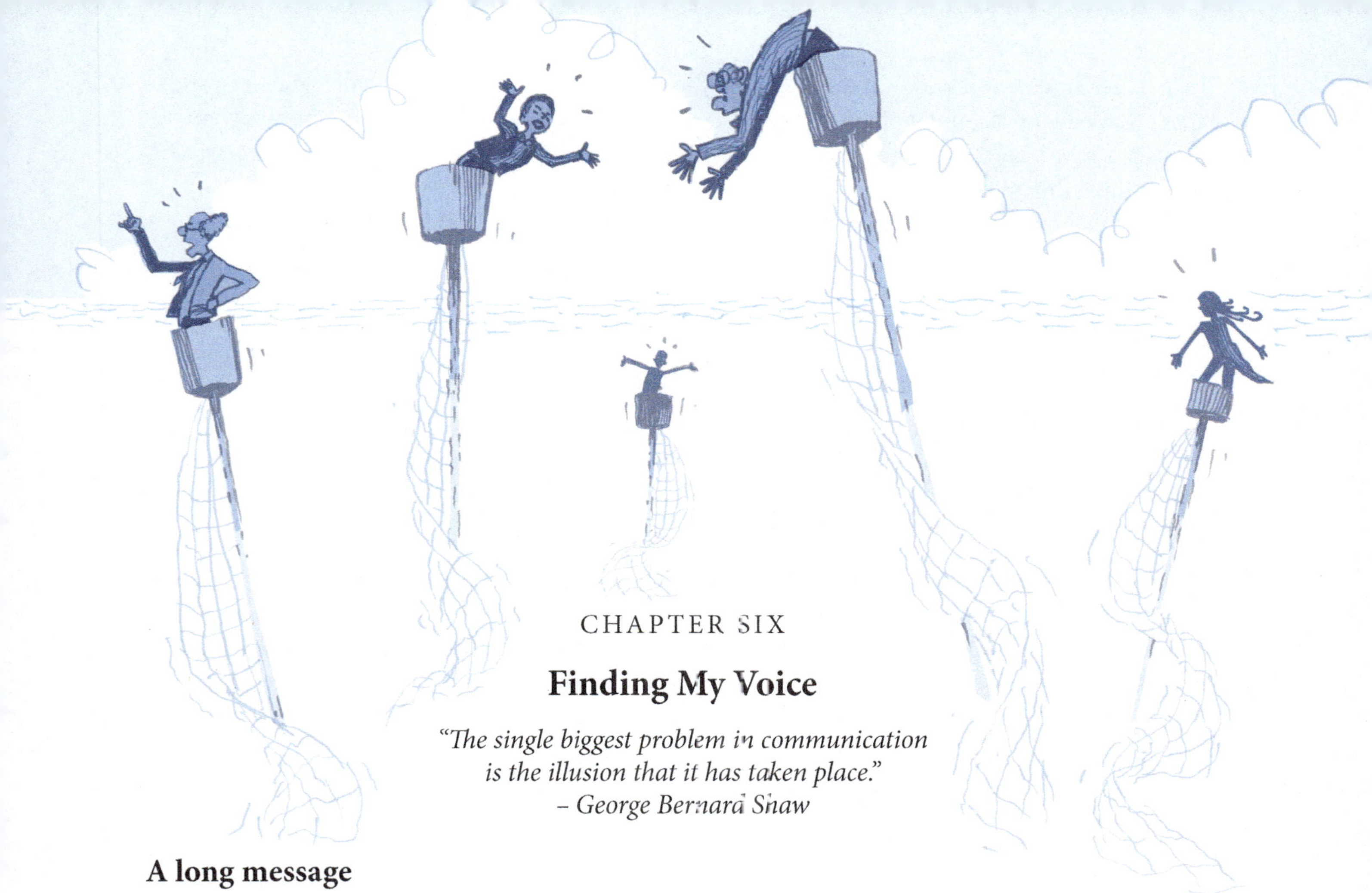

CHAPTER SIX

Finding My Voice

"The single biggest problem in communication is the illusion that it has taken place."
– George Bernard Shaw

A long message

John began his career as a lawyer. He practised commercial litigation and environmental law at one of Canada's biggest law firms in Toronto. The pace, as you might imagine, was frenetic.

One evening, when he was still a junior lawyer, John was working late on a case at the office. As he was finishing up, he decided to leave a voice message for the senior partner responsible for the file. So, he hit the record button and talked. And talked and talked. When he had finished, he packed up and headed home.

The next day, John went to see the senior partner to get his input on the issues that John had raised in his message. When John asked him, he was surprised by the answer.

"I don't know what you said. I stopped listening after 30 seconds and deleted the message."

John looked at the partner, not sure what to say.

The partner smiled and said, "Sit down. Look, you cannot leave a five-minute voice message and expect that anyone is going to have the patience to listen to it or that they will remember what you said. You're a lawyer. Language is your tool. You have to communicate clearly and persuasively. You wouldn't dream of leaving such a meandering message for a client; you wouldn't submit a brief to the Court of Appeal with paragraphs that ran on for pages. Don't do it with me or your colleagues here at the firm."

It was a powerful lesson on the importance of good communication.

Advice from a car salesman

Lee Iacocca, the former Chairman of the automobile company Chrysler, said, "You can have brilliant ideas, but if you can't get them across, your ideas won't get you anywhere." The ability to communicate your ideas in a manner that is clear, memorable, and that motivates people to take action and get the job done is a critical skill for any individual.

Finding your voice is not a crusade to let the world know who you are. It is a more subtle process of discovering what you want to say, and then learning how to say it. Becoming an effective communicator takes time and effort, but it is easier than many people think. And it is worth the effort. Those who have the confidence to communicate usually have many more opportunities for professional and personal growth than those who don't.

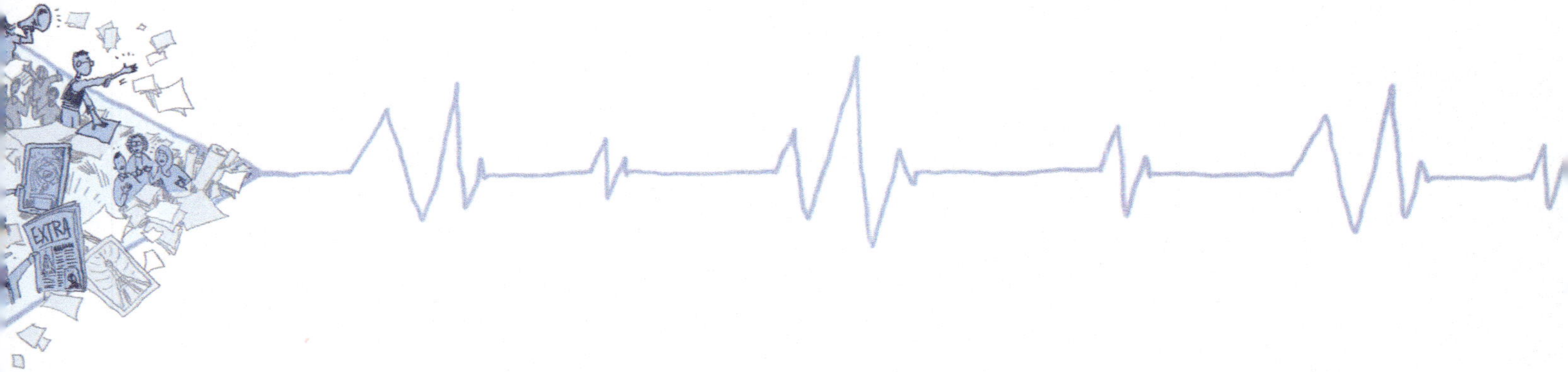

Communication: The lifeblood of a healthy work environment

Blood is essential for our survival, and it is constantly being circulated. Oxygen-depleted blood enters the heart from the body and is pumped to the lungs where it is reoxygenated and sent back to the heart to be pumped out to the body.

The average heart beats around 100,000 times per day, pumping approximately 7,200 litres of blood every twenty-four hours. Your heart is pumping right now—we hope! Try this: with the index and middle fingers of your left hand, find your pulse on your right wrist.

If you work in a medium-size or large organization, there is a good chance that each time you feel your heartbeat, another type of communication has taken place in your company. Phone calls, meetings, memoranda, reports, text messages, Slack updates, hallway conversations. And don't forget email, although given that most people send and receive well over one hundred emails each day, we doubt that you will.

It all adds up to a lot. The challenge is to cut through the noise and get to the heart of meaningful, effective communication.

You don't need a transfusion, just better communication skills

Communication can be likened to the blood in our bodies. It circulates, flowing upward, downward, and laterally, carrying vital information from one part of the organization to another. When our blood is healthy, it flows smoothly. It delivers oxygen and nutrients to our cells and takes waste products away from our body's tissues. However, if we have a blood disorder, it can affect our overall health.

If you do not work on your own communication skills, over time, it can have a negative effect on your career and your ability to make an impact. It can also have a negative impact on your self-confidence. Good communication skills help build and strengthen good relationships which have a positive impact on our mental well-being.

Companies like Microsoft, LinkedIn, Fast Company, and others have conducted surveys in which they asked heads of companies and organizations which skills they look for in potential future leaders of their company or organization. Consistently, at or near the top was the ability to communicate well.

No matter what your position is, you must be a communicator. There is no getting around it.

Make good communication a priority and commit to working at it.

If good communication is so important—and if most people understand that it is important—why is there so much poor communication? Unfortunately, there is no easy answer.

The reasons for poor communication

Poor communication is the result of different factors, or a combination of those factors.

Lack of confidence

Communication is stressful for many people. The amount of stress can change depending on the subject being discussed, the context in which the communication is taking place, and the people with whom you are communicating.

This stress does not appear only for a speech or presentation. Many people lack confidence when speaking in less formal situations, such as speaking up at meetings, chatting with people at social events, or even calling a business to complain about a product or service.

Why do we lose our confidence when we speak? It could be fear of judgment, fear of forgetting what we want to say, fear of making a mistake, or something else. This lack of confidence is something that can be compounded by the technical aspects of speaking.

In a November 26, 2021 blog post, author and business expert Seth Godin wrote:

> "It's pretty clear to me that our speaking voice is not the result of the inevitable physical evolution of our vocal cords. It's something our brain figured out how to do with the part of our body that keeps us alive by breathing.
>
> "And because it's a late addition, there are a bunch of kinks in the system.
>
> "Talking while breathing is the beginning of the challenge.
>
> "But it's also worth noting that the entire process is in the middle of a huge number of sensitive muscles and nerves. This means that when we're talking (calling attention to ourselves) we're also trying to keep all of that stress at bay. Add microphones, Zoom, and the high-stakes world of being seen, and you can start to understand why it's so easy to get hoarse, to sound like someone you're not, to develop tics, to amplify your stress, and a whole host of other challenges.
>
> "If you don't sound like you, it might simply be because your brain is sabotaging the thing you're trying to say. I used to riff about 'no one gets talker's block' but now I'm not so sure. I think most of us do."

What about you? How do you feel when you give a presentation or have a crucial conversation or speak up at a meeting? Is your ability to share your ideas hampered by any limiting beliefs? What, if anything, is holding you back?

Lack of motivation

When it comes to communication, many people lack the necessary motivation to do a good job. Often, this lack of motivation stems from a mistaken belief that they have nothing to say. Or, perhaps, they feel that they have something to say but that their words will not make a difference. So, why bother?

The problem with a lack of motivation is that the longer it persists, the more entrenched it becomes. If you find that you lack motivation to communicate from time to time, go back to the exercises in Chapter 3 on motivation. And remember, if you do not share your ideas, you might be missing an opportunity to make a positive difference in the lives of others. This idea of focusing on the recipient of your message rather than yourself is something which we explore in greater detail below.

Lack of clarity

Being able to communicate in a manner that is clear is a crucial skill. Too often, however, people fail to devote appropriate attention to the way in which they communicate, and the message is muddled. This lack of clarity can lead to a number of communication mishaps.

At the micro level, it means that people do not know what is expected of them because those in leadership fail to provide clear instructions or just assume that people know what they are supposed to do. At the macro level it means a lack of clarity about the organization's purpose or where things are headed.

Have you ever received a communication—written or verbal—and you were not clear what was being requested? Have you ever had people ask you to clarify one of your own communications because it was not clear?

Aggressive Communication

In the worst cases, a person's communication style might be arrogant, condescending, or even intimidating, any of which could easily lead to a toxic work environment. Such people do not talk to or with others, they talk at them.

Sometimes it is because the person with whom they are speaking has an aggressive personality and they believe that this is how to show strength and get ahead. Sometimes, however, a person might not be aware that they are being perceived as aggressive. Is it possible that you have, on occasion, been aggressive in your communication style? Have you ever sought feedback on this point? It is never a bad idea to seek advice from those whom you trust.

Cultural issues

We live in a global world.

We are more connected to each other than ever before and as the world gets smaller, work environments are becoming more and more culturally diverse. It is not unusual to find individuals from different cultures, languages, races, religious beliefs, and gender identities working closely together.

Working in a culturally diverse workplace is an enriching experience. Learning from others who have different perspectives and sharing your perspectives with them brings with it the potential for a dynamic and creative work experience. But it also brings challenges, particularly regarding communication.

People from different cultures do not always see the same things in the same way and they do not express themselves in the same way. For example, something as simple as a smile could signal delight in one culture but embarrassment in another. Likewise, a certain gesture could be a sign of encouragement in one culture and a vulgar symbol in another. And what might be considered aggressive in one culture might be normal in another.

When people from different cultures communicate, the risk of miscommunication increases. This is especially so when the communication takes place in a language that is the mother tongue of one of the speakers but not of the other. Native speakers often use idioms and colloquial expressions that are hard for non-native speakers to understand. Many non-native speakers are at a disadvantage when it comes to expressing themselves. Words that might seem harsh or blunt could simply be the easiest way for them to express themselves. Perhaps you have experienced this challenge yourself if you speak more than one language.

And don't forget that cultural differences can also exist between professions; they can arise between people in different departments within the same firm. For example, it is not uncommon to hear people in the marketing department complain that salespeople do not understand them, while those in sales say the same thing about the marketers.

Poor listening

There is a saying that because we were born with two ears and one mouth, we should listen twice as much as we speak. Happily, there are many who follow this advice; unfortunately, there are also those who have it the other way around and speak twice as much as they listen.

However, even the best listeners among us have a frequent, or at least occasional, bad habit: we listen to respond instead of listening to understand. What do we mean?

Have you ever been in a meeting with colleagues to discuss a particular issue? You come to the meeting with your ideas and sit down at the table. One of your colleagues starts presenting his or her thoughts on the issue. You start listening and at some point, while your colleague is still speaking, you begin formulating your response in your mind. You have stopped listening and started thinking. Your colleague is still talking but you have zoned out and might be missing something of relevance.

The environment

Finally, the environment in which you find yourself can have a major impact on the health of the communication in your company or organization. Are there "safe spaces" in which people can express themselves freely and without fear of retribution? When people feel that they can share their views openly and that they will not be penalized for doing so, the atmosphere is lighter and more productive. This is the essence of psychological safety that we discussed in Chapter 1.

The costs of poor communication skills

When the blood in our bodies is anemic or not circulating properly, the consequences can be severe. Likewise, the consequences of poor communication can have costs and repercussions, not just for an organization, but for you personally.

Poor communication skills can have a huge impact on the quality of any desired outcomes. They may result in the message being lost or misunderstood, or in the speaker being labeled as a poor communicator.

From missed opportunities to being misunderstood, the cost of poor communication skills can often cascade in a domino effect. However, take heart, it does not have to be this way. Good communication is possible, it just takes a bit of effort and a slight change in perspective.

What is good communication for you?

Good communication has a number of elements, and once again, we are confident that you instinctively know what many, if not all, of them are.

EXERCISE: Effective communicators

Take a moment to think about the people whose communication style you admire. They could be famous people, people in your office, or family and friends. Why are they effective? What do they do? What are the characteristics of effective communicators?

Characteristics of effective communicators

We are willing to bet that your list did not include things like a person's age, culture, or sex. You did not say that an effective communicator needs to be a certain height or weight, or that they have to make a certain amount of money. All of the things that you listed are things that can be learned and improved if you are willing to make the effort.

EXERCISE: You as a communicator

But this book is not about other people, it is about you. So, what would you say about your own communication skills? What are the things that you think you do well as a communicator? What are the areas that you would like to improve? What others told you?

Two things to keep in mind as you complete the table below:

- It is important to get feedback from others on your communication skills, because after all, what counts is how your communication is received.
- After you have completed the scrolls below, ask yourself whether any limiting beliefs have influenced how you responded.

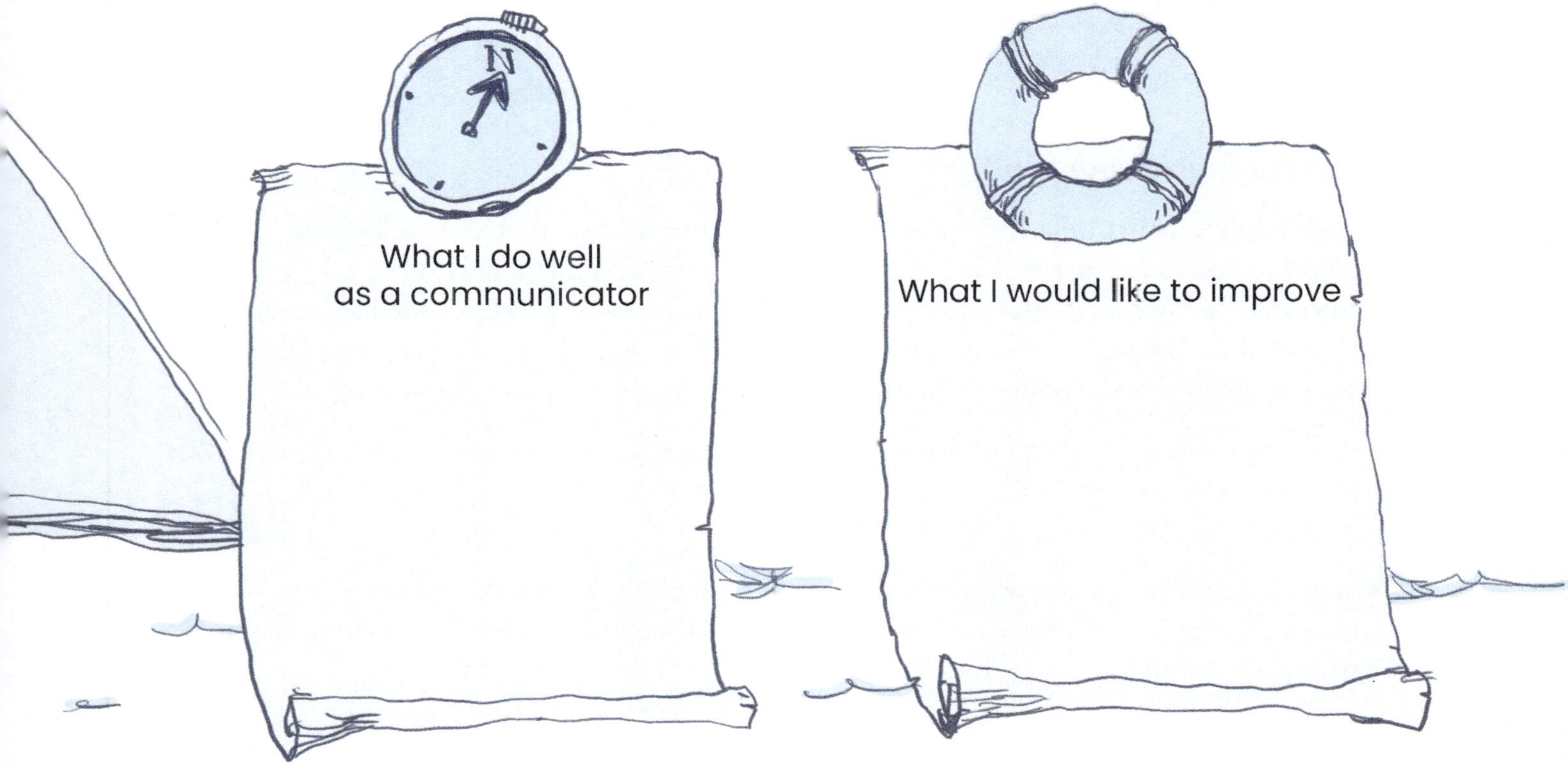

You can become a good communicator. If and when you do improve your communication skills, you will see opportunities open up, personally and professionally. You have to work at it consistently, but the investment is one that will pay dividends for years to come.

Recognize your responsibility

Too often, people expect others to understand what they have said or written. Being that presumptuous often stems from the fact that we all suffer from something known as the curse of knowledge. In essence, it means that when we know something so well, we tend to forget what it was like when we knew nothing at all about it. Because we forget, we mistakenly think that what is obvious to us will be obvious to those with whom we are communicating.

For example, a doctor who has performed one thousand surgeries can forget what it was like when he had never performed a surgery. A lawyer who has argued hundreds of cases can forget what it was like when she had never argued a case.

Often when we communicate, we are speaking about something on which we have spent a significant amount of time. Thus, concepts or expressions or ideas that are obvious to us might not be obvious to others.

Remember that when you communicate an idea to others, it is your responsibility to ensure that the idea has been received and understood. Think carefully before speaking or writing; think about what you want to say and what you hope to achieve. And once you have communicated your idea, do whatever is necessary to ensure that your message has been understood.

The big picture

There are three key components to any form of communication whether it is written or verbal: the person initiating the communication, the recipient of the message, and the message itself. If you don't have all three, there is no communication.

Here is a 4-step process that you can do the next time you are preparing an important communication.

1. Understand the situation

On a sheet of paper, draw a triangle. At the top, write the name of the person initiating the communication who, in all likelihood, is you. At the bottom left of the triangle, write the subject of your message and at the bottom right of the triangle write the name of the recipient who will receive it. If you are delivering an important message to your teammates, you don't have to list all their names, just write something like "Team."

Now, think about the three relationships between the points on the triangle and make notes along the sides of the triangle about each. Below are examples of some questions you might ask about each relationship:

Me–Message: What is the one thing that you want the recipient to remember, even if they forget everything else? Why are you communicating the message? What do you know about it? Why is it important for you? What insights can you share with the recipient? Do you have all the information necessary to communicate in a clear, open, and honest way?

Recipient–Message: Why is the message important for the recipient? What does the recipient know about the message? Is it something that is new for them or do they already have experience with it? Do they like the subject? Do they not like it?

You–Recipient: What is your relationship with the recipient? Is it a constructive relationship or is there some "baggage" that either or both of you are bringing to the conversation? Are you speaking to your boss, subordinates, or a client?

Once you have made your notes, you need to consider a fourth element and how it might affect your analysis, i.e., the situation or the context in which the communication is taking place. For example, is this an all hands company meeting? Is this a meeting to discuss the team's performance on an existing project? Is this an annual performance review? Is this a meeting in which you are going to raise an uncomfortable issue with your boss?

Here are some questions to ask when thinking about the context in which the communication will take place:

- How does the situation affect the message, if at all?
- Will the situation affect the way in which the message should be delivered?
- What will happen for you and the recipient if the communication goes well?
- What will happen if it goes poorly?
- What is at stake?

The purpose of this first step is to get as clear a picture as possible of the key components of the communication. It forces you to step back and think about the "big picture" before narrowing your focus.

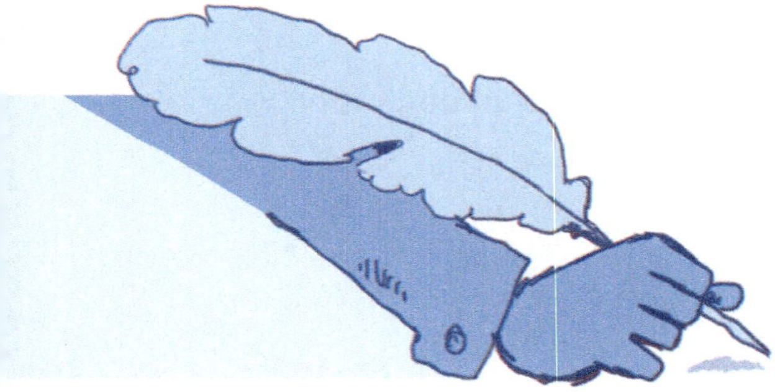

2. Define your objective

What is your objective for the recipient of your message? What should happen once the communication has taken place? What is the concrete outcome you seek?

Some possible objectives for a business communication: (a) you want the recipient to take some action; (b) you want the recipient to change some behavior; (c) you want the recipient to be aware of certain information; (d) you want the recipient to bring about some change in the company.

Sometimes the initiator just wants the recipient to know something and that is fine. However, the most powerful communications are the ones that move people to action. If you can get people to take some concrete action, you will have made an impact.

When thinking about what you want the recipient to do, be specific. Write out the objective as follows: "Once communication has been made, [name of recipient] will ________________."

There are countless objectives that your communication might have, so give it some thought. Just remember that the objective should be clear and realistic. The people with whom you are communicating need to know what is required of them, and they have to be able to do it.

3. Be clear about your message

Earlier in this chapter, we discussed the importance of clarity. Your message should be clear to those who receive it. Ideally, every communication has a single message. The more messages you have, the more complicated your communication; the more complicated your communication, the less likely that people will understand it.

Think about what you want the recipient to remember once they have listened to you or read your email. Then, write out your message in a single, grammatically correct sentence; don't use bullet points. When you can condense your message into a single sentence, the message will likely be clear in your mind. When the message is clear in your mind, there is a greater likelihood that it will be clear to the recipient.

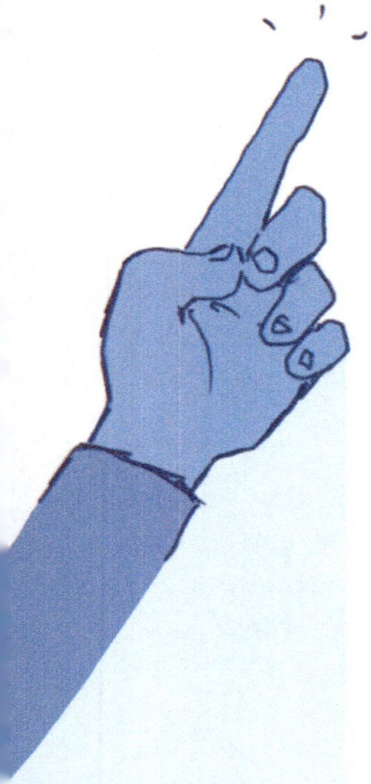

4. Make the message relevant

The message of any communication—whether a presentation, email, or conversation—should always be relevant for the recipient. If the message is not relevant, it is a waste of everyone's time.

The final step of this exercise is to be clear about how your message is relevant for the recipient. In order to have a meaningful basis for communication, you need at least one reason why the people with whom you are communicating should care.

We are not suggesting that you go through this 4-step process every time you have to speak with a colleague or send an email; it would be far too cumbersome. Instead, use this exercise for important communications. Nevertheless, for any communication situation, pausing for a moment to think about your objective, your message, and its relevance for the recipient will help ensure that your communication is meaningful the next time you speak or click "Send."

Speaking of which …

Think before hitting "Send"

Just when you thought you would make it through a self-development book without having to read about emails! Unfortunately, they have a major impact on the way in which we communicate. The statistics vary, but there is general consensus that in 2020, more than 300 billion emails were sent every day. You read that correctly, 300 billion, with a "b." Every. Single. Day. That number is projected to grow significantly in the years to come.

Many studies show that the average office worker spends more than two hours a day reading and responding to emails. The vast majority of those emails, including cc's and bcc's, are not relevant to their job. Let's put these numbers into sharper focus. If you spend two hours a day reading, writing, and responding to emails, over a forty-year career, you will spend more than 29,000 hours or 3.33 years on emails!

Before you think that we are exaggerating, let's do a short exercise. Put the book down and open your email. How many messages are sitting in your inbox? How many of those have arrived since you last checked your email? How many of those messages are neither relevant nor helpful?

When you add all the messages that you receive on social media platforms such as Slack, WhatsApp, Instagram, LinkedIn, and others, the sheer amount of information that comes flooding in is overwhelming.

Many people respond like a Pavlovian dog when they receive a new email or social media notification. They stop what they are doing and open the message. Their work is disrupted, and time is lost. Brain scientists have shown that constant task-switching is challenging for the brain. If we stop working on Task A to focus on Task B (such as a new email), when we eventually return to Task A, we are not operating at the same level of efficiency. We need to mentally "downshift" and get started up again. It takes time.

When deciding to send an email, we encourage you to consider the following factors in this order:

- Is it necessary to send this email at all?
- How concise can I make this email?
- Who are the only people who must receive this email?

As a final incentive for you to use email judiciously, did you know that your emails have a major environmental impact? All those emails in Outlook or Gmail are stored on servers. Those servers require a lot of energy to operate, and all that energy has an impact on the environment.

Sending fewer emails is not only better for communication, it is better for the planet!

Be culturally aware

There is a Korean proverb that says, in essence, two people looking at the same mountain from different sides will not see the same thing. It is wisdom worth heeding. Different cultures value things differently and people from different cultures express themselves differently.

How can we improve our cultural awareness? If you communicate frequently with people from different cultures, spend some time reading up on those cultures. Not only is it interesting, but it also shows respect on your part and will help you communicate more effectively with your counterparts.

Ask them to tell you a bit about their culture, especially customs pertaining to business. Ask them what they think of business etiquette in your culture. A sincere desire to learn more about them will shine through. You will learn and they will feel that you care about them. It will be *Sawubona* in action.

It is also important to remember that people from different cultures value principles and ideas differently. A principle that is extremely important in one culture might be less important, relative to other principles, in another culture. How important these principles are for a culture has an impact on how people from that culture communicate.

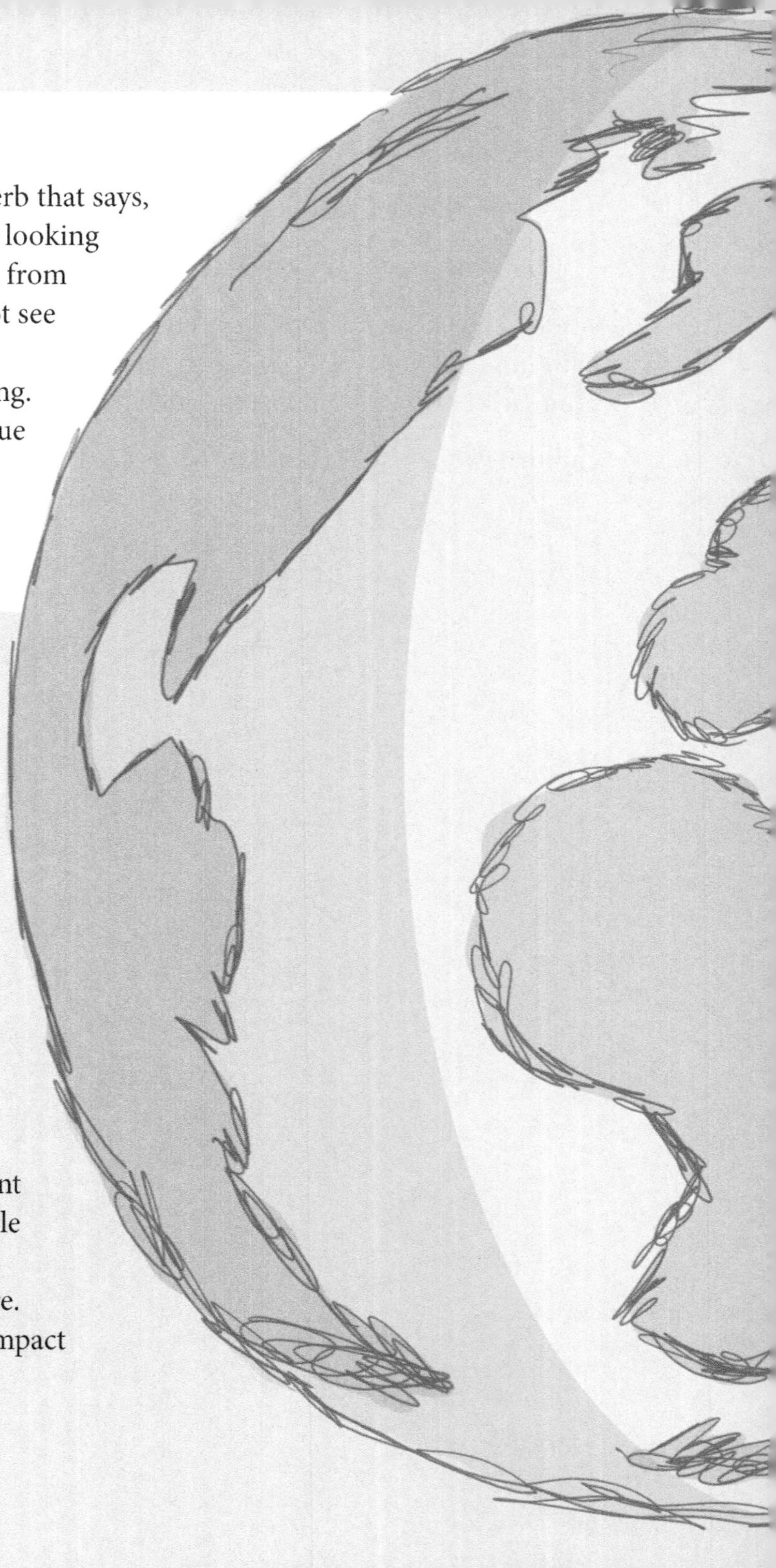

An exhaustive analysis is beyond the scope of this book, but to take one example, a person from a culture that places high importance on individual effort and low importance on power distance (the relationship between an authority and subordinates) will likely communicate differently at work than someone raised in a tradition that values collectivism and respects large power distances.

If you wish to learn more, one good resource is the work of Geert Hofstede. He was a social psychologist, IBM employee, and Professor Emeritus of Organizational Anthropology and International Management at Maastricht University in the Netherlands. Hofstede is famous for his research on cross-cultural groups and organizations.

And remember, even though we are different from each other in many ways—physically, linguistically, culturally—our differences are small compared to what we have in common. The values that you worked on in Chapter 3, the ones that you hold dear, are shared by people around the world. They are the bridges that can span the linguistic and cultural gaps between people.

Illustrator's story

On his first trip to Asia in 2007, Kevin traveled to Tokyo with a team of business consultants. While preparing for the trip, Kevin and his colleagues were captivated by the allure of the East; however, none of them knew anything about the formal Japanese traditions and protocols for everything from the exchange of business cards, speaking in meetings, sitting, and even eating soup!

Determined not to be undone by a cultural faux pas, Kevin and his team scoured various resources for advice and guidelines to bridge cultural differences so that they could communicate and accomplish their objective. Not content to just watch YouTube videos or review a list of "do's and dont's", they had several pre-departure meetings, ran through possible scenarios in improvisational rehearsals, and asked experts to evaluate their performance.

The practice paid off. The experience in Japan was successful, even though there were occasional embarrassments and slipups. After his return to the United States, Kevin recounted some of his missteps to a Japanese friend. "Oh, you did that?" his friend said before continuing, "Don't worry, they'll forgive you. They're all Buddhists."

There's always more to learn.

Difficult communication

Not every conversation will be easy. Sometimes, you will have difficult conversations: about a person's performance; about a problem; about a dispute with a colleague. While these situations are not necessarily pleasant, the communication can be much more effective when the parties involved follow a few principles.

- Focus on issues, not personalities. The purpose of the conversation is to resolve a problem. Keep your eyes on the prize.
- Ask questions as often as you make statements. A difficult conversation usually involves multiple points of view. Your position should be heard and respected, but so should the position of the person with whom you are speaking. Listen to understand and ask if anything is not clear.
- Be open-minded. Is it possible that you have overlooked something?
- Think critically about your position as much as the other person's. If you are open-minded, it will be easier to think critically.

- Recognize that the parties to the discussion might not have the same information. Many difficult conversations arise because the parties involved have unequal access to information, which itself might be the sign of poor communication. Make sure that everyone has, and can agree on, the same facts.
- Defend your position respectfully. Of course, you should stick up for what you believe is right but there is no need to attack another person while doing so. An ad hominem attack is disrespectful and counterproductive.
- When you are wrong, admit it. You are not perfect. You have made and will continue to make mistakes. Admitting when you are wrong is a sign of maturity and strength. It is also much more productive.
- Try to find common ground. The more common ground you find, the stronger your footing will be and the greater the likelihood of resolving the problem effectively.

Simple messages

Albert Einstein said that if you can't explain something simply, you don't understand it well enough. By that standard, it seems that many people do not understand what they are talking about. Why is this so?

There is no one answer. In some cases, people feel the need to talk about everything. In others, they have not thought carefully about what they want to say, or they do not have a clear understanding of the issue. This is why we have spent so much time in this chapter stressing the responsibility that you have as a communicator and the reasons why it is important to be clear about what you want to say.

In our experience, communication often fails when people try to cover too much, and in too much detail. The result is muddled for the recipient of the message. If you know what your message is, stick to that and significantly reduce anything that does not relate to that message.

Simple words

Winston Churchill said, "Broadly speaking short words are best and the old words when short, are best of all." It's a shame that more people do not follow this advice.

Why do we complicate our communication with vague terminology or redundant words? Why do we "reach an agreement" when we could just "agree?" Why do we "utilize" things when we could just "use" them? Why do we talk about "strengthening interdepartmental synergies" instead of clearly explaining what we want people to do?

Simple words are easy to understand. They leave less room for misinterpretation. Nobody will think that you are unintelligent if you use simple words in your communications. Does this mean that you can never use a complex word? Of course not. But the bulk of your communication should be comprised of simple words.

(Did you notice that last sentence? We should have said: "Simplify most of your communication.")

Listen up

Imagine a bridge that spans a rushing river. You are on one side and your colleague is on the other. You each see the river, but from different perspectives. While you may be looking at the same thing, you do not see it the same way.

You want your colleague to cross the bridge and see things from your perspective, so you wave them over. But they want you to see things from their perspective and are signalling for you to come to their side. If you are each insistent, you may well end up standing on your respective sides of the bridge trying to shout above the noise of the rushing water. What if there was a different way? We once saw the following exercise during a corporate training that highlights this common dilemma.

An instructor arranged two rows of chairs facing each other. Participants each took a seat across from another participant. The instructor then said that the objective of the exercise was for the participants to convince their counterparts to get up and stand behind their chair. In other words, between participants A and B, A would win if B stood behind A's chair and B would win if A stood behind B's chair. Of course, hilarity ensued.

Most people begged and cajoled their counterparts to stand behind their chairs. They talked about how beautiful the view was from their perspective, they offered to buy lunch for their partners and generally tried all kinds of ways to get their partners to move short of picking them up and carrying them! The secret to the game, however, was much simpler. The "winning" pair of participants agreed that each would get up and then stand behind the other's chair.

It is a good metaphor for communication. What if, instead of stubbornly sticking to your position, you met in the middle of our metaphorical bridge? There, you could speak clearly, openly, and honestly. Perhaps you could then "walk" together to one side and then back to the other. In this way, you could each share your perspective but also better understand the perspective of your colleague.

Listening is 50% of communication. One person conveys an idea and the other person listens. If nobody is listening, there is no communication. And yet, how often do we truly listen to what other people are saying? Chances are, not very often.

The next time you are in a meeting, observe how often people are giving their undivided attention to the person who is speaking. Are they looking at them? Are they nodding in agreement? Are they making notes of key points?

Or do they exhibit other behaviors? Are they checking their smartphones? Reading material? Having a side conversation with someone else? Are they leaning back, visibly bored, or gazing longingly out the window?

Now, flip the lens around: Are you sometimes guilty of these behaviors? If so, why not commit to doing better. Before your next meeting, commit to putting your phone on mute and leaving it in your pocket. Commit to not looking at it during the meeting. Instead, focus on your colleagues.

Listen to understand

Above, we noted that when people are interested in what is being discussed, they still often do not listen properly. This is because they are listening with the intention of responding; instead, they should be listening with the intention of understanding. What is the difference?

When people listen to respond, once they have heard enough information to know what the person is talking about, they start thinking about what we want to say in response, even while the person is still speaking. Have you ever been guilty of this habit? Most people, including us, have.

You are in a meeting, listening to someone express her opinion about why, for example, the budget for a certain project should be cut. But you think the budget should, in fact, be increased because you believe in the project. So, as your colleague is laying out the reasons to support her position, you start formulating the reasons for the counterargument.

That means you are no longer listening to her. Are her reasons valid? How would you know? You have stopped listening. A person cannot actively listen and plan a response at the same time. Thus, you may miss some important piece of information that would justify the budget cut.

Not only can you miss important information, but this bad habit shows a lack of respect for the person who is speaking. Flip the situation around. Would you not like people to listen to what you have to say? Right until the end? Would you not like people to understand and think about what you have said before they offer their own opinion? Courtesy is a two-way street.

A listening exercise from the world of improv

How can you improve your active listening? Here is an exercise from the world of improv. The exercise is called "Last Letter–First Letter" and the rules are simple. Two people have to create a story together. It has to be a coherent story. Each person can only say one sentence at a time. Then, it is the other person's turn. Back and forth, they build the story together.

The key rule is as follows: The last letter of the last word of one person's sentence must be the first letter of the first word of the other person's sentence. So, for example, the story might begin as follows:

- Once upon a time, a king lived in a castle on a mountain.
- Nobody knew what the king looked like because he was so reclusive.
- Everyone was afraid of him.
- Mostly everyone, but not a little girl named Rachel.
- "Look," said Rachel to the villagers, "maybe he is afraid of us."

For a modified version of this exercise, the two people can have a conversation instead of creating a story. Thus, for example:

- How are you today?
- Yesterday was better.
- Really? What happened?
- Did you hear about the proposed changes in the team structure?
- Everyone's talking about it; are you directly affected?

During applied improvisation workshops for business, trainers will often do this exercise. It is not always easy for the participants, especially if the last letter of your partner's last word is a "k" or an "x," but the exercise is always humorous and fun. The real insight, however, comes during the debrief at the end of the exercise.

The trainer asks the participants how they found the exercise. The typical response is that people found it fun but challenging. And then comes the trainer's big question: "Yes, it can be challenging, but did you find that you were listening to the other person right until the end? Without thinking about what you were going to say?"

In almost every training in which we have been involved, it is a light-bulb moment. The looks of astonishment demonstrate what a revelation this exercise is for people. They realize that they actually were listening completely, without trying to formulate their next sentence.

You can try this exercise the next time you are having a conversation with someone you know well. You don't even have to tell the other person that you are doing it! Just listen to what they are saying right until the end. Then begin your first sentence with the last letter of the last word that they said. (We don't recommend that you try this out for the first time in an important meeting. Better to practice with friends or family at lunch or a similar gathering.)

You might be surprised at how good it feels to actively listen to someone else. And they might be surprised at how attentive you are!

Listening for what has not been said

Thus far, we have focused on actively listening to what people say. That, of course, is important. But it is also important to listen for what is not said.

There is an ancient Chinese legend about a king who sent his son to learn wisdom from the great master, Pan Ku. No sooner had the prince arrived at Pan Ku's temple than Pan Ku sent him alone into a nearby forest. Pan Ku told the prince to stay there for one year and then return to the temple and tell what he had heard.

One year later, the prince returned and told Pan Ku everything that he had heard: birds singing in the trees or screeching in the sky; leaves and grass rustling in the wind; cicadas singing; bees buzzing; wolves howling; badgers growling; and more. Pan Ku listened patiently and then told the prince to return to the forest to find out what else he could hear.

As you might imagine, the prince was not too happy about this. He had just spent a year in the forest and was looking forward to sleeping in a comfortable bed! He had told the great master everything that he had heard and now he had to return and listen some more. Nevertheless, he obeyed and went back to the forest.

There the prince remained a few weeks more. At first, he only heard the same sounds as before. But then, one day, as he sat quietly, the prince began to hear other, subtler sounds that he had not heard before. He realized that these were the other sounds that Pan Ku had wanted him to hear.

The prince hurried back to the temple and Pan Ku asked him if he had heard anything else. The prince replied, "When I sat quietly and listened carefully, I heard sounds that I had not heard before. I could hear the sound of the sun as it rose in the east; I could hear the soil warming up in its golden rays; I could hear the sound of plants growing; I could hear the sound of ants marching along a fallen tree; I could hear the sound of a butterfly landing on a flower. These were all sounds that I had not heard before."

Pan Ku nodded and smiled. He said, "You have done well. Being able to hear the unheard is critical for anyone who wants to communicate well. You must cultivate the ability to listen to what people do not say. You must listen for what they keep in their hearts, the feelings that they repress and the fears that they do not express. When you can do this, you can communicate in a manner that instills confidence and elicits support for your ideas."

Don't worry, we are not going to ask you to go sit in the forest for a year although, as we discussed in Chapter 4, a walk in the forest every now and then is good for you on many levels. But we do encourage you to listen deeply for what people are not saying. Go back and review the story of Joe and Matt beginning on page 44, and the related exercises, as a reminder of how you can improve your skill at listening for what has not been said.

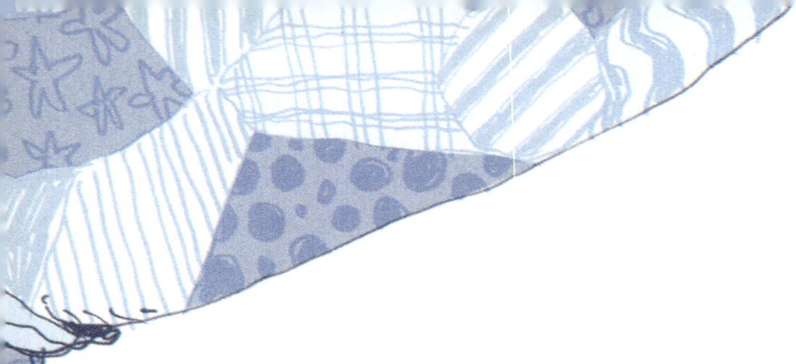

Finding your voice

How do you find your voice? It is all about taking the time to reflect on who you are and what you stand for.

- What is important to you?
- What are your values?
- What do you believe?

You have already done a lot of work on these questions in the previous chapters. You have taken the time to reflect on your values and motivations, and the kind of impact that you want to make in your work life. You have explored ways in which to build on your strengths, overcome limiting beliefs, and use your creativity and innovation in your work life. You have gained clarity on your aspirations and what you want to achieve in your life.

As a result of this work and reflection, you probably have thoughts and ideas that you want to share; thoughts and ideas that can make a difference to your company, your clients, your community, and perhaps even beyond. You have something to say but that is not enough.

One step at a time

If your aspirations are going to become a reality, you are going to have to influence others. You have to know how to say it. Whether you are in a leadership position or part of a team, it is critical that you be an effective communicator. Indeed, effective communication is the soft skill that is valued most by the leaders of companies and organizations.

But it is not always easy. It takes courage to voice one's opinions, especially when there is a chance that those opinions will be criticized or even rejected. Add to this all the things you need to remember when communicating and it can all feel a bit overwhelming. Do not despair; take it one step at a time.

Once you have identified the values that are important to you, work on incorporating those values in your communication. For example, if honesty is one of your personal values, be honest in your communications. If inclusiveness is important to you, seek the input of others when you communicate.

Practice makes progress

Becoming an impactful communicator is something that takes time and practice. The best way to become a good speaker is to speak.

It is not a linear process. You will make progress but you will also have setbacks. Has the following scenario ever happened to you? You may have an important meeting, presentation, or conversation for which you prepare extensively. You arrive at the event and say what you have to say. Afterwards, you realize that you could have said something differently, or come up with a better response to a question.

The French have a great expression for this situation. They call it *l'esprit de l'escalier*, literally the spirit of the staircase. It refers to thinking of the perfect thing to say after the event is over and you have left. Don't worry, it happens to everyone (and more than once). Enjoy your successes but embrace your failures or missed opportunities and learn from them.

As you progress, look for ways to develop your communication skills and self-confidence. Seek out opportunities to give presentations and speak up at meetings. Have you ever had an idea while sitting in a meeting but were too timid to share it? And then, someone else spoke up with the very same idea and everyone else liked it? How frustrating is that?

Join a public speaking organization such as Toastmasters International where you can practice your speaking in a supportive environment and get feedback that will help you improve. Speak at events in your community. Attend seminars and watch videos of great speakers.

Every time you speak, you gain a bit more experience and a bit more knowledge. Over time, it all adds up.

Some advice about feedback

We are not always the best judges of our capabilities, and our perceptions are not the same as those of others. Getting feedback is an important part of your development as an effective communicator.

You do not always have to wait until after you have spoken; be proactive. If you know that some of your colleagues will be in the audience for your presentation, ask them to look for things that you did well and areas where you could improve. Have them consider both content and delivery. People will be more open to giving you meaningful feedback if you give them permission beforehand.

And here is a tip: Do not ask for *feedback*; instead, ask for *advice*.

Daniel Pink, best-selling author of books such as *A Whole New Mind, Drive* and *The Power of Regret*, says that people are often reluctant to give feedback because they don't want to be critical. However, everyone loves to give advice. And advice is actionable because when people give advice, they will suggest concrete things that you can do.

Once you have received this advice, reflect on it with an open mind. Although you do not have to accept it, resist the urge to reject it immediately. Take some time and then, if you still do not agree, you can disregard it. However, if different people keep giving you the same advice, it is usually a sign that you should consider it carefully.

Finally, take all the advice that you get and prioritize it in terms of what to work on. Do not try to change everything at once because that rarely goes well. Instead, pick one thing and work on it in your next presentation, meeting, conversation, or interview. When you have mastered that skill, move on to the next thing. Remember, improving your communication skills is a lifetime endeavor; it is a marathon, not a sprint.

You've got style

We all have our own style of communication. For example, some people are loud and impassioned; others are quiet and measured. The reasons for our different styles of communication involve our upbringing, education, and more, something we discussed in Chapter 3.

At the same time, you have to remember that you are not a single-dimensional person. You have a range of emotion and energy and you do not speak the same way on every occasion. For example, think about how you speak in different situations, such as when giving a corporate presentation, during a team meeting, or when you go out with friends.

Unfortunately, we cannot give you a magic pill that will help you plug into the right speaking style for every occasion. It does not work that way. Finding your style comes down to practice and experience. Once you have found it, it becomes a matter of knowing how to "adjust the dial" depending on who your audience is.

Ultimately, it is about heeding the words of the Irish writer Oscar Wilde: "Be yourself. Everyone else is already taken."

Be emotionally smart about it

As you work to find and develop your voice, do not forget the importance of emotional intelligence. Do not forget the concept of *Sawubona* that we discussed on page 51. The people with whom you are communicating have their own ideas and are living lives that are just as complex as yours.

Here are six principles of emotionally intelligent communication that can guide you as you use your voice throughout your journey.

Always remember the words of the American poet and civil rights activist, Maya Angelou: "I've learned that people will forget what you said, people will forget what you did, but people will never forget how you made them feel."

A final thought

Finding your voice does not mean that you have to become a great orator. However, you must be able to express yourself in a manner that is clear and compelling, especially with regard to those values that you hold most dear. Finding your voice will help you make the impact that you were born to make.

Once you have found your voice, you will have found a rudder to help keep your ship in your flow channel. You will have mastered a skill that will help you bring about the changes that you want to see in your world. Even so, it is important to recognize that your voice will only get you so far.

In 1922, German author Hermann Hesse published his classic novel, *Siddhartha*. It is the story of a wealthy young Indian who rejects a life of privilege to seek spiritual enlightenment.

Siddhartha, the hero of the novel, leaves his comfortable life as a Brahmin and sets off on a journey that sees him, over the course of his life, as an ascetic in the woods, a wealthy businessman with a beautiful courtesan, and a simple ferryman on a river. It is only after going through a lifetime of trials and tribulations that Siddhartha achieves enlightenment.

Near the end of the novel, Siddhartha meets Govinda, his childhood friend who has also been on his own spiritual quest. Unlike Siddhartha, Govinda has yet to attain enlightenment and he asks Siddhartha to tell him what he has learned and how he went about doing so. Siddhartha responds by saying that of the many thoughts that he had had over his life, the most important one was that wisdom cannot be communicated. Every person has to find it on his or her own.

Knowing the limits of communication is one of the most important lessons about communication. Ultimately, people have to experience and learn things for themselves.

We can share with others our knowledge, our vision, our strategy, and our standard operating procedures, and they can certainly learn something about them on an intellectual level. However, it is only in the doing that they will learn the wisdom of such things.

Thus, when you are communicating with others, remember that you can only take them so far; they must finish the journey themselves.

CHAPTER SEVEN

Decisions, Decisions

"Once you make a decision, the universe conspires to make it happen."
– Ralph Waldo Emerson

Now what?

In the introduction, we asked you a question: Why did you pick up this book? If you have made it this far, we hope that you have found some answers.

Along the way, we have given you a lot of homework and a lot to think about, from being yourself to working with others; from finding motivation to developing your full potential; from letting your creativity flourish to communicating with conviction. All of this thinking is important. As Socrates said, "The unexamined life is not worth living."

However, if all you do is think, nothing will get done and there will be no progress. As we noted in Chapter 5, you have to act, and in order to act, you have to make decisions. When you get down to it, life is all about decisions.

The cut-off point

When we decide, we choose from different alternatives. Deciding to go with one option means that we have decided to not to go with others. We have cut off those options. In fact, the root for the word "decide" can be traced back to the French word *décider*, which means to settle a matter. That word, in turn, comes from the Latin *decidere* which is composed of the words *de* meaning "off" and *caedere* meaning "cut." So, in a very literal sense, when you decide, you are cutting off all other options.

We make hundreds of decisions every day: what to wear; what to eat; whether to read a book or watch Netflix; whether to open that email or focus on the task at hand; whether to stay where you are or make a move.

Not all decisions are the same. Some are easy: whether to drink coffee or tea. Some are difficult: whether or not we should accept a new job offer. What distinguishes one decision from the other are the potential consequences.

If you order a meal and do not like it, the experience might be unpleasant, but it will not be life changing. You can eat something different at your next meal. However, if you accept a job, it can change the trajectory of your career, and indeed, your life.

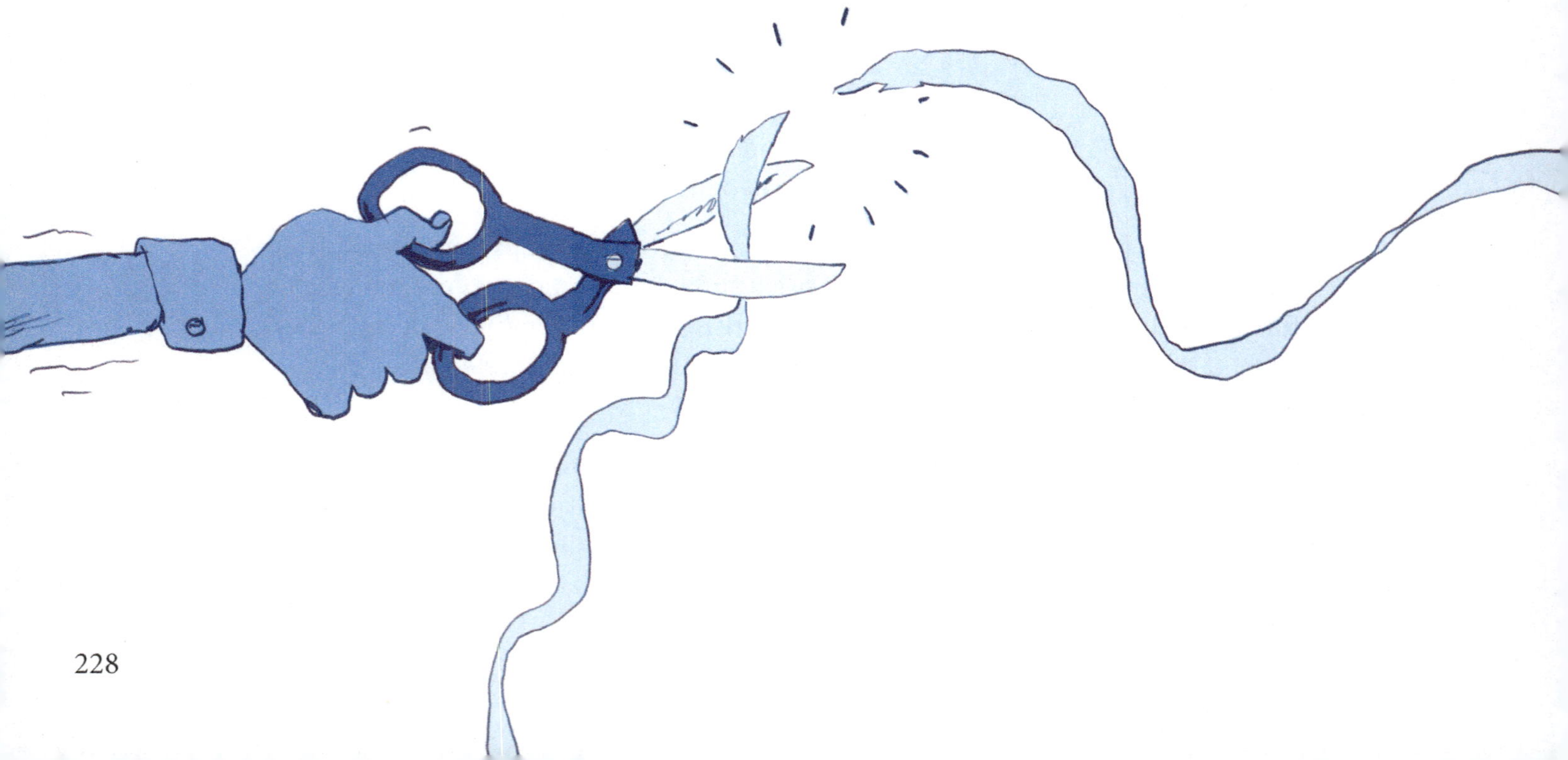

"Highly illogical," said Mr. Spock

Whether your decisions are banal or life changing, how much are they driven by logical thinking? Reflect on that question for a moment.

We might think that we make decisions by logically ruling out options to arrive at the best choice. However, we would be wrong. Many studies have concluded that emotions play a huge role when we make our decisions. Indeed, they are an integral part of the decision-making process.

Many experts agree that more than 80% of our decisions are based on emotions and instincts, and less than 20% are based on logic. Studies of people with injuries to the part of their brain where emotions are generated show that these injuries affect their ability to make decisions.

As noted above, when we decide, we choose from different alternatives. However, we cannot choose if our emotional system is broken. Our logical thinking will only take us so far in our deliberations. We need our emotions to get us to make the actual decision.

Understanding this important human (as opposed to Vulcan) characteristic is extremely valuable, especially when we are faced with a major decision such as whether to accept a job offer or promotion.

Make a decision

In this chapter, we look at decision-making. How do you make decisions about your work life, especially when those decisions impact others? What are the obstacles to good decision-making? How do you react to decisions made by others that affect you, especially when you do not agree with them?

More importantly, this chapter is about helping you to make the most important decision of all. Will you continue as you are, or will you make a change? If the latter, how big will that change be? Are we talking about minor adjustments to your work-life journey, or do you need to take a new direction (and possibly a new ship)?

Whatever your course of action, it should begin with a thoughtful decision based on a sound consideration of the different options and understanding what is in alignment with who you are and where you are headed.

And remember, not deciding is itself a decision. As the Canadian rock band Rush sang, "If you choose not to decide, you still have made a choice."

EXERCISE: Decisions you have made

Before we take a deep dive into the decision-making process, think of two or three important decisions that have influenced your life trajectory, positively or negatively. These decisions can be from your personal life or from your professional life. They can be recent decisions or ones that you made years ago.

What did you take into account when you decided? How did you feel?

My decision	How I made the decision	How I felt while deciding	How I felt once I decided	My core values that were involved	Impact of the decision

Do you see any patterns in your decision-making process? Maybe you do a detailed analysis during decision-making, or you consult with trusted friends. Perhaps you imagine the impact of the decision and how it will change your life. Maybe you set out all the pros and cons.

As you reflect, which do you remember more clearly: the details of a logical process or the emotions that you felt during the process? What observations can you make about yourself and how you decide?

Challenges to good decision-making

By doing the above exercise you might have discovered something about your decision-making regarding the things that are important for you. Even when you understand your purpose and what motivates you, and even when you have a clear idea of the contributions that you want to make, it can still be difficult to make the decisions related to your career.

Let us look at some of the challenges and what you can do about them.

Uncertainty

Perhaps the biggest challenge of all is uncertainty. You can never be 100% certain that your decisions will work out the way you hope they will. As Steve Jobs said in his 2005 address to the graduating class at Stanford University, you will only be able to connect the dots of your life in the future when you are looking back in time.

A lack of uncertainty can lead to several consequences.

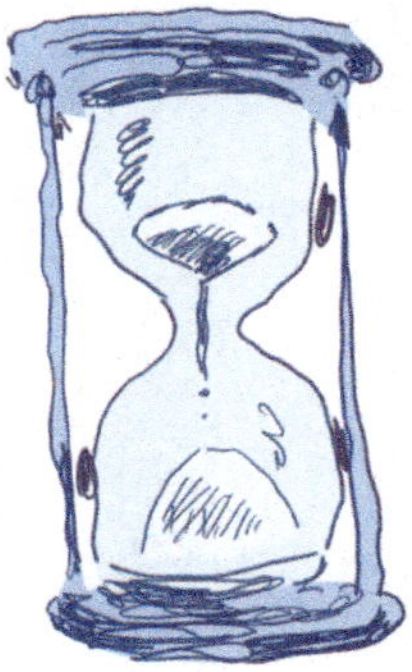

- You might delay or even avoid making a decision. While thoughtful consideration of alternatives and possible outcomes is good, prolonged delay or avoidance rarely works out in the long term. Issues that were problematic before can become significantly worse over time and you might find yourself forced into a decision under pressure.

- You might start to overthink the issue. This can lead to the dreaded "analysis paralysis" in which you find yourself with too many variables to consider and an inability to decide. Psychologists have studied the effects on our thinking when there are too many options, something we look at more closely below.

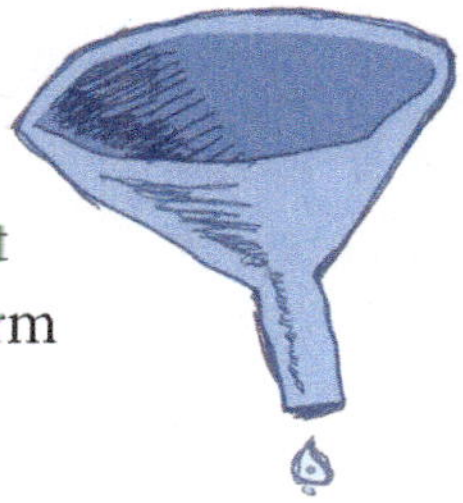

- You might oversimplify the issue. This outcome is the opposite of the one above. It can result in not considering key factors or only thinking of short-term considerations instead of the long view.

Bias

We all have cognitive biases. Some of them take time to develop and others can be based on a single experience. But biases can become significant roadblocks when it comes to making decisions. They can skew your ability to think about an issue objectively by bringing in external factors that have little or nothing to do with the decision itself.

There are many different types of biases, for example:

Confirmation bias: This bias is the tendency to look for and interpret information in a way that confirms or supports your previous beliefs or values. You have an idea as to how things should be and so you actively seek out evidence in support of that idea while downplaying or disregarding evidence that contradicts your beliefs or values.

Overconfidence effect: When you believe that your abilities or judgment are better than they are, you are suffering from the overconfidence effect. In 1980, Ola Svenson, a professor from the Department of Psychology at the University of Stockholm, conducted a now famous study in which he asked groups of Swedish graduate students and American college students to assess their driving ability relative to their peers. In response, 69% of the Swedish students said that they were better than average and 93% of the Americans said that they were better than average.

Hasty generalization: When you rely too heavily on a single reference point to justify your decisions, you are making a hasty generalization. The reference point could be a single piece of information or a single experience. For example, many people refuse to fly on certain airlines because they once had a bad experience with that airline (delayed flight, rude flight attendant, etc.). However, thousands of other travelers might love that airline.

Halo effect: The halo effect occurs when your positive impressions about one characteristic of a person or thing leads you to form positive impressions about other aspects of that person or thing. Social media has greatly increased the impact of the halo effect. We see people sharing photos of themselves looking great in exotic locations and we tend to assume that they must be happy and successful when the truth is usually much more complex.

Noise

Daniel Kahneman, the Nobel Prize-winning psychologist and economist has spent much of his career studying decision-making. He maintains that bias actually plays a small role when it comes to decision-making. For Kahneman, the concept of "noise" is more important. As human beings, we are imperfect decision-makers, and our judgment is affected by a wide range of factors.

At a fundamental level, your culture, your religion, and your upbringing can have a significant influence on how you make decisions. However, your capacity for effective decision-making can also be impacted by ordinary factors such as how hungry you are, whether your favorite sports team won or lost its last game, whether you are breathing clearly or are congested, whether you had a good night's sleep or not, whether the weather is sunny or cloudy, etc.

All of this "noise" can impact your decision-making abilities. Indeed, Kahneman says that when it comes to decision-making, humans are not particularly good. In his award-winning book *Thinking, Fast and Slow*, he says that we would be better off relying on an algorithm to come up with the right decisions in a wide variety of different situations.

Too many options

Have you ever found yourself with too many options? At best, it can slow you down in the decision-making process; at worst, it can stop you in your tracks and lead to what is often called the "paradox of choice."

Author's story

John was born in Canada but now lives in Switzerland. Whenever he goes back to Canada for a visit, he always stops by the pharmacy to stock up on products that he cannot get in Europe.

On one such occasion, John wanted to buy a certain deodorant. He rounded the corner of the relevant aisle and walked to where the deodorants were stocked on the shelves. A man was standing in the aisle, staring at a wall of deodorants and antiperspirants. There were dozens of brands and fragrances. John stood beside him and looked at the shelves.

"There sure are a lot of different deodorants," John said.

The man was silent for a moment, then let out a sigh and responded, "There are too many," he responded, "I can't decide." And he walked away empty handed.

Studies have shown that when people are offered too many different choices of a product, they will buy less often than those who were only offered a few. Even if you do buy in the face of lots of choices, there is a good chance that you will think about the choices you did not make and experience "buyer's remorse." Have you ever had this experience?

The extent to which you will be happy with your choices is directly related to your ability to compare the costs and benefits among the different options. When there are too many options, it becomes impossible to make all of the comparisons.

EXERCISE: Challenges to decision-making

How would you assess your challenges to decision-making?

	Often	Sometimes	Rarely	Never
Delay or avoid decisions				
Overthink decisions				
Oversimplify decisions				
Confirmation bias				
Overconfidence effect				
Hasty generalization				
Halo effect				
Noise				
Too many options				

You have now looked at some of the main challenges to good decision-making and thought about your own approach. How can you improve and make even better decisions in the future? There are strategies that successful decision-makers use. Let's explore some of them now.

How to be a better decision-maker

Aside from flipping a coin, how can you become a better decision-maker? There are things that you can and should do.

Understand what motivates you

When it comes to making decisions, you always hope that your decisions work out for the best. You seek pleasure, reward, and fulfillment, and you want to avoid pain, disappointment, and loss. That is understandable. However, what constitutes pleasure, reward, and fulfillment for one person will not be the same for another. You must decide what is important for you.

For example, investors must make decisions about where to invest their money. They have a finite amount of money and cannot invest in everything, so they have to decide. One investor might be focused on maximizing return and thus be prepared to take more of a risk. Another investor might have had a bad experience in the past by losing money to an unscrupulous company. In the latter case, the investor might be willing to forgo a "moonshot" investment opportunity for the security that comes with investing in a more trustworthy, stable company.

In this book, you have explored the importance of motivation and how it drives you to meet your needs. You have thought deeply about your values and aspirations. By now, you should have a clearer idea of what gets you out of bed in the morning to go and do whatever it is that you do.

Recognize the decision-making environment

Do you remember that queue in the supermarket and the likelihood that you have added something to your purchases (chewing gum, breath mints, a magazine) while waiting in line to pay? There is a reason why stores place these kinds of items near the checkout (and why so much candy is conveniently placed at the eye level of children).

This phenomenon is known as choice design or choice architecture. The term "choice architecture" was coined by Richard Thaler and Cass Sunstein in their book, *Nudge: Improving Decisions About Health, Wealth, and Happiness*. It refers to the way in which an environment is set up to nudge people to make certain choices. You are exposed to different choice architectures all the time. Look no further than the Internet.

Have you ever decided to discontinue receiving an email newsletter and had to hunt around for the (very small, grey) "unsubscribe" button? Have you ever visited a website and found that it is very easy to accept all cookies but rather challenging to opt out of all non-essential cookies? These, and thousands of other, systems are designed to lead you to make (or not make) certain choices.

How can this help you with your own decision-making? Why not design your own system for making better choices? For example, you could establish a rule that between 9:30 and 11:30, you will not check email or social media but will instead focus on productive work. To improve your health, you could commit to not eating anything after a certain time in the evening. Before you waste any more time in meetings, you could decide that you will only attend meetings where you have decision-making authority or can contribute or are interested in the subject.

Strengthen the decision-making muscle

Making decisions is something at which you can get better. It is the same as strengthening your muscles by going to the gym. When you first start going to the gym, you will not likely start by bench pressing 225 lbs (102 kg). Instead, you will start with lighter weights and build up your muscles over time.

Similarly, you can start to train your decision-making muscle by not agonizing over minor decisions. At the grocery store, don't spend a lot of time trying to decide which box of cereal to buy. Just pick one and go with it; if you do not like it, you can buy something different the next time. Apply this tactic to dozens (if not hundreds) of other items when shopping for groceries.

Take the same approach with other, relatively minor, decisions: the restaurant where you will eat; the movie that you will watch; the hotel or Airbnb where you will stay. The more decisions you make with confidence, the more confident you will be in making decisions, especially when the stakes are higher.

Reduce the number of decisions you make

Let's stick with the muscle-building metaphor a bit longer. To strengthen your muscles, you need to work them out. However, if you overwork them, you will become exhausted and might even injure yourself. Therefore, you need to balance exercise with rest. The same holds true for decision-making.

The term "decision fatigue" was popularized by the journalist John Tierney. It refers to the fact that our ability to make good decisions becomes weaker with every passing decision that we make. This idea has been explored in detail in several books such as *Willpower: Rediscovering the Greatest Human Strength* by Tierney and Roy Baumeister, and *The Power of Habit: Why We Do What We Do in Life and Business* by Charles Duhigg.

If you start your day having to decide what suit to wear, what tie to wear, what outfit to wear, what to eat for breakfast, whether to go for a run before or after work, which bus to catch into town, etc., you are already drawing down on the daily bank of decision-making credit. It might be imperceptible, but your ability to make decisions during the day becomes a bit weaker with each decision that you make.

This phenomenon is, perhaps, most noticeable at the end of a long day during which you made several important decisions. You arrive home and know that you should do some exercise and eat a healthy supper, but you are tired—more mentally than physically—so you decide instead to order a pizza and settle down to watch some Netflix.

We are certainly not averse to taking in a good movie and eating a pizza now and then. But for many people, pizza (or some other fast food) and Netflix are more than a now-and-then event.

Successful people limit the number of trivial decisions that they make so that they can focus on what is truly important. It is why Steve Jobs almost always wore a black turtleneck, jeans, and New Balance running shoes every day. It is why Mark Zuckerberg wears a grey T-shirt and jeans most days. Zuckerberg has said, "I really want to clear my life to make it so that I have to make as few decisions as possible about anything except how to best serve this community."

When he was President, Barack Obama almost always wore a blue suit or a grey suit. Obama said that he was trying to limit the number of decisions he had to make. As President, he had to make momentous decisions and he did not want to waste energy worrying about clothes or food. Obama was committed to having routines that allowed him to focus on the important things.

How can you reduce the number of decisions you have to make in a day? One way is to turn decisions into routines or habits. Habits—both good and bad—are powerful because we do not have to expend energy to make a decision; we just act. Brushing our teeth in the morning is a habit; for many people, reaching for their smartphone when they wake up to check social media is also a habit.

Are there any areas in your life where you can eliminate a decision? Are there any areas where you can establish a routine so that it will become a habit? For example, what if you had the habit of turning off the phone, computer, and television one hour before you went to bed? You would likely get better sleep and be more energized the next day.

If you have the liberty of dressing like Jobs or Zuckerberg, perhaps you can simplify your wardrobe. If not, perhaps you could take five minutes on the weekend to decide what you will wear each day of the week so that, on the given day, you know exactly what to pull from the wardrobe. Or what about having the same (healthy) breakfast every morning so that you do not have to spend time wondering what to eat.

The fewer the decisions, the more brain power you will have for the important decisions.

Limit your options when possible

Limiting the number of decisions that you make is great, but ultimately, you are going to have to make some. Sometimes the decision will be between two options; for example, two job offers. Sometimes there will be several options from which to choose. In such cases, whenever possible, reduce the number of options as much as possible.

We have talked about overwhelmed consumers in the face of too many options. Some companies have understood this reality and reduced the number of products on offer. The results were dramatic. In the 1990s, Proctor and Gamble reduced the varieties and sizes of its famous Head & Shoulders shampoo from twenty-six to fifteen and sales increased by more than 10%. Similarly, by reducing the number of products that it sold, Costco also increased its profits. There are many other examples of companies profiting by giving their customers fewer options.

Whenever you can reduce the number of options for a decision, do so. It will be easier to compare the relative pros and cons, and thus it should be easier to reach a decision.

Put yourself in a box

We hear so much about "thinking outside of the box" these days and yes, it is good to allow yourself to be creative and inspired when trying to solve problems. That is what Chapter 5 was all about.

However, when it comes to decision-making, going in the opposite direction can yield benefits. Sometimes, putting yourself in a box can lead to better decision-making.

What kind of a box? Well, it could be an actual spatial box. Not a box like the one you played in as a kid after an appliance was delivered to your parents, but rather a room or other defined space. Corporate teams often do this when they have to make a decision by bringing all of the stakeholders together. In the era of COVID-19, these rooms have often been virtual.

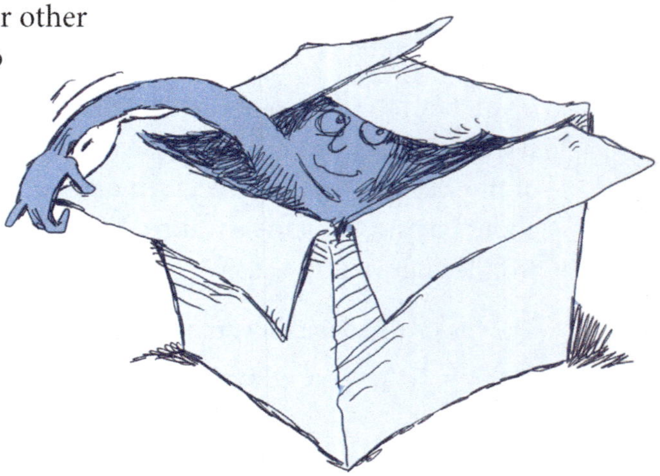

You can also put yourself (or your team) in a time box and set a deadline by which a decision must be made. Deadlines work well when it comes to focusing the mind. Did you ever put off studying for an exam or finishing a paper when you were in school? We bet that the looming exam date or deadline submission got you to act!

Gather necessary information

Note the word "necessary" in the title above. We are drowning in information these days and there will always be more that you can read.

In the opening stanza of his classic poem, *The Rock*, the American poet T. S. Eliot wrote, "Where is the life we have lost in living? Where is the wisdom we have lost in knowledge? Where is the knowledge that we have lost in information?" Eliot wrote those words in 1934, a long time before the Internet and social media came along to give us unlimited access to infinite information.

Not all information is necessary to make a decision. Indeed, you will often lack information but still have to decide. That is why some decisions are hard, you cannot know the outcome. For example, accepting a promotion is an exciting step in your career, but it often comes with doubts and insecurities as to whether you are up to the task. In such cases, it can feel safer to stick with what you know.

Gather only whatever information is necessary, whether through documentation or by soliciting the input of key stakeholders. It will help you assess the relative merits of your different options, which as noted above, will facilitate the decision-making process.

Check your blind spots

If you have learned how to drive a car, one of the things that you probably learned early on was to check your blind spots. You can see much of what is going on behind you by glancing in the rearview mirror or the side mirrors. But you cannot see everything.

When driving, we have blind spots over and slightly behind each shoulder. Before changing lanes, it is crucial to check your blind spot so that you do not cause an accident. You should also check your decision-making blind spots.

Early in this chapter, we noted some of the challenges to good decision-making. At some point in the process, it is always worthwhile to stop and ask yourself, "Am I missing something?" Doing so can help clarify your thinking.

If you are having trouble with your self-assessment, ask a trusted friend or colleague. Be specific in your request. Do not ask them what they would do, rather, explain your thought process as it currently exists and ask them for their opinion on whether there might be something that you have missed or not considered.

Make a decision

It might seem like common sense that one of the steps in the decision-making process is to actually make a decision. However, as the French philosopher Voltaire said, "Common sense is not so common."

After deliberating and weighing the pros and cons, make a decision and go with it. Will it always turn out perfectly? Of course not. Life does not come with an ironclad guarantee. But a decision brings closure to one process and opens possibilities for something new.

Furthermore, continuously putting off a decision can have damaging implications for individuals and teams. As you continue to deliberate, morale ebbs and it feels like you are treading water, which after a while, becomes exhausting. And when you think about it, if you continuously put off a decision, you are, in fact, deciding. You are deciding to do nothing and although that can sometimes be the right decision, it usually is not.

Make a decision and then adjust as things play out. You may be familiar with the phrase, "Ready, aim, fire." For too many people, this becomes, "ready, aim, aim, aim, aim …" with no "fire." The best approach is "ready, aim, fire" and then, if necessary, adjust your aim and fire again.

EXERCISE: Daily decisions

List the decisions that you make every day before 12:00 pm. Think of as many things as possible, even if they might not feel like a decision; for example, brushing your teeth, checking your email, deciding what to wear and how to travel to work, etc. Each of these actions is preceded by a conscious decision on your part to perform them.

Once you have your list, rate each decision on a scale of 1–5 in terms of its importance, with 5 being extremely important. Focus less on the decision itself and reflect on what would happen if you did not make that particular decision. For example, if you usually drive to work, what would happen if you did not have a car?

As you do this exercise, it should become apparent just how many decisions you make every day and how many have simply become subconscious habits. Think about how many of these decisions are still serving you well today and make a conscious decision—yes, another decision—as to whether you wish to maintain, change, or stop it.

You may find that deciding to walk to work instead of driving may give you more time to exercise, discover new areas of your neighborhood, and maybe even meet more people. Did you notice any correlation between the decisions with the greatest level of importance and the values you hold dear?

Making a decision that impacts others

As you advance in your career, there will likely be more people over whom you have direct authority. You will be responsible for their work, and you will have the power and obligation to make decisions that affect them. Not every decision will be popular, but that comes with the territory.

Be clear about the process

In the previous chapter, we explored the importance of communication and how to find your voice. When it comes to decisions affecting others, communication is crucial.

Of course, not all decisions are equally important, and not all decisions require consultation and debate. Nevertheless, when making a decision that has an impact on others, the best situation is one in which people can be informed about the process as it unfolds.

If the process allows for input from others, be clear about how that input will be received and considered. If you cannot or will not consider input from others, it is better to be up front about that in the first place rather than give the false impression that you want to know what other people are thinking.

Along the way, be sure to keep people informed. As we saw on page 83, this is exactly what Barry-Wehmiller did with its employees during the 2008 economic crisis. Uncertainty is never a good thing in the corporate world. It is stressful and provides fertile ground for rumors and speculation. Uncertainty is a void, and a void tends to be filled.

Therefore, as the decision-making process unfolds, keep people apprised of the situation. If a date for a final decision has been fixed, let people know. People will appreciate the fact that they are being kept informed.

Announce and explain the decision

Once a decision has been made, those affected should be told as soon as possible. Some decisions can be conveyed via email while others are best done live, whether in person or online. In the case of significant decisions affecting large numbers of people, an announcement could be sent via email and followed up with a town hall meeting for questions and discussion.

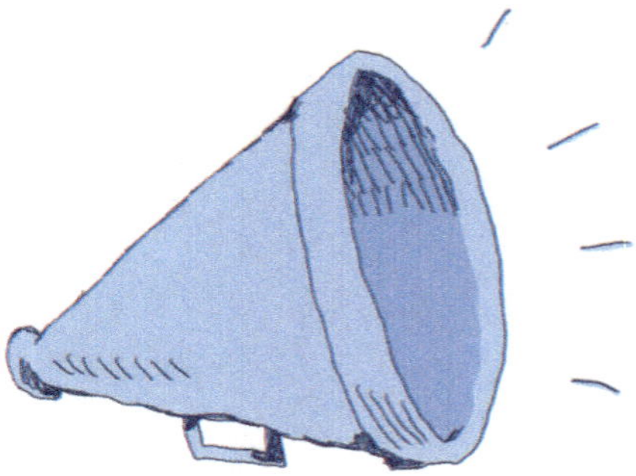

Make sure that people understand the rationale for your decision. Especially in cases where you know that some people would have preferred an alternative option, take the time to acknowledge those people and how they feel. Demonstrate how you considered their preferred option, and why, after weighing the pros and cons, you chose an alternative.

People will not always be happy with your decision, but they will be less unhappy if they feel that their viewpoints were considered carefully.

Dealing with the decisions of others

Thus far, we have been discussing your decisions. It is worth spending a moment to consider decisions from another perspective. How do you handle decisions made by others that have a direct impact on you?

If you work in a company or organization and are not at the pinnacle of power, there will be times when you are subject to the decisions of others. Sometimes you will agree with those decisions and sometimes you will not. The former situation is easy to handle, the latter less so.

How do you respond to decisions with which you disagree? Do you grumble to your co-workers? Do you half-heartedly go along with the decision? How you react in such situations speaks to your character and will influence how other people see you.

It is important to distinguish between two types of decisions. The first type is one that goes to the heart of what you stand for as a person. If your company has decided to do something with which you fundamentally disagree, such as paying unfair wages to workers in developing countries, disregarding the environment when designing a manufacturing process, or branching out into sectors such as tobacco or weapons, it could be a signal that you should start looking for work elsewhere.

Fortunately, most corporate decisions are of a second type. They will, for the most part, relate to matters such as corporate strategy or allocation of resources, hiring, or promotion matters. This is not to say that such things are not important, but rarely do they require deep introspection as to whether you should continue working for the company or organization.

So how should one handle a decision with which one disagrees? There are a few things that you should, and should not, do.

First, do not gripe about it, especially if you are in charge of a team that looks to you for leadership. Workplaces around the world are filled with enough negative watercooler talk; you don't need to add to it. You are part of an organization and have to accept that you will not always agree with every decision.

Next, recognize that you might not be aware of all the factors that went into a decision. Have certain services been reduced or cut? Perhaps there were financial constraints. Has an investment been made in an area where you do not see value? Perhaps those who made the decision had information that you did not.

Once you acknowledge that you might not have all the information, look at the decision from the side of those who were in favor of it. In high school debating, it is a common practice to give students a topic and have them argue one side in one debate and the other side in the next debate. Doing so not only trains their advocacy skills, it also broadens their thinking and helps them think more objectively about issues in general.

With regard to the decision that you oppose, what are the benefits? What is the upside? Stepping back and thinking about things from the opposite viewpoint often puts things in a whole new perspective.

The biggest decision of all

How often do you spend hours or even days debating whether you should make a purchase of something that, in the grand scheme of things, is not important? And yet, when it comes to profound questions such as where do we want to work, you jump at the first opportunity that comes along?

Choosing how and where you decide to deliver your unique value in your work life requires introspection and thought. It requires at least as much time as you will spend deciding whether to buy a computer or a pair of shoes.

Of course, when thinking of making a major change, it is important not to act hastily. Giving yourself enough time to think about your situation and consider the merits of your different options can lead to a more beneficial outcome.

It is important not to confuse a temporary funk or malaise that we all go through from time to time, with being stuck in an untenable position. In fact, when you find yourself wondering about your future, take some time and write down your thoughts and feelings in your Idea Book that we introduced in Chapter 5. It is a simple form of journaling. Every day, for a few weeks, you make three entries: one as soon as you get up, one at midday, and one at the end of the day. For each entry, you answer a simple question: Do I feel fulfilled? You can expand on your answers with reasons why or why not.

At the end of the period, review your entries. Do you notice any patterns? How often did you feel fulfilled or unfulfilled? What provoked these feelings? The purpose of journaling is to get you to reflect on your life from both an emotional and an analytical perspective. It can help you get clarity on what should stay the same and what should change.

EXERCISE: Making better decisions

Think back to the exercise on page 231 when we asked you to come up with two or three decisions that you had made in the past and reflect on the things that you took into consideration when making those decisions.

Now think about the insights you have gained from this chapter about making better decisions. Is there anything that you could have done differently about the decisions that you made? Are there any lessons that you apply to your future decisions?

In the illustration below, write what you have learned about your decision-making process on the waves behind the boat.

On the waves in front of the boat, write what you can do about your decision-making process in the future.

A final thought on decisions

Making a decision can be scary. As we said at the beginning of the chapter, when you decide, you cut off all other options. You might not be burning bridges, but you might find it hard to cross back over. That is all part of making a decision.

Life does not come with a guarantee, except that it will end. There is no way to be 100% certain that you are making the right decision. However, if you have a clear vision of what you want to accomplish in life, the process of making decisions becomes easier.

Once you have considered all the factors that are important to you, make your best decision and go with it. You will receive feedback along the way that will help you navigate the turbulent waters that will inevitably arise. Do you honestly think that there will come a time when you never have any more problems?

In this book, you have explored your values, your intrinsic motivation, and your purpose. The work that you did in the previous chapters to frame your current situation and to focus on the things that you want to achieve should have helped in this regard. Having come this far, your vision of your future should at least be somewhat clearer. If so, you will have some decisions to make. Use the tools that you have discovered in this book and the insights that you have gained to help you with those decisions.

And remember, not everyone will agree with what you decide. People, including those who care about you, may call you foolhardy or reckless or crazy. That is not always easy to handle, and doubt might set in. Ultimately, however, you are responsible for your own life.

It is not for us to tell you what to do now; only you can decide how you want to continue your work-life journey as you enter your flow. Nevertheless, be mindful of the seductive allure of always playing it safe. As Sir Richard Branson, a man who has made a number of incredible decisions in his life, says, "The brave may not live forever, but the cautious never live at all."

CHAPTER EIGHT

Continuing Your Journey

"If you are brave enough to say goodbye, life will reward you with a new hello."
– Paulo Coelho

Your journey has begun!

Having a clear understanding of your personal purpose and ensuring that it aligns with the work that you do is essential for a fulfilling life. Moreover, it will provide intrinsic motivation to master your areas of expertise and make the best possible impact on the world. This fulfillment, and the contributions that you make, are the key components for your success, satisfaction, and happiness.

Your organization and your working environment can have a positive influence and help you to thrive. However, you cannot just rely on your work life to provide you with what you need. The challenge that this book addresses is to ensure that you are in control and can chart your personal career journey in the direction that you want to go.

Having read this far, you can already identify many of the ingredients that contribute to your ideal work-life journey. Now that you have taken a comprehensive view of all these elements, it is time for you to act.

Your personal transformation

We believe that you already have the curiosity and determination to explore and discover how to achieve greater fulfillment and happiness from your work life. This is just the beginning of your transformative journey as you enter your flow channel.

It would be easy to put this book back on your shelf and focus on other pressing issues in your life. If that happens, there is a good chance that what you have discovered will not develop any further. At best, it will be retained as a dim thought-provoking glow of interest. At worst, it will fade away.

In the film *Up in the Air*, George Clooney's character works for a company that specializes in helping other companies downsize and fire their employees. He is an expert at what he does. He handles difficult situations with calm professionalism and is often able to convince people that being fired is actually a chance to take stock and focus on the positive opportunities that lie ahead.

In one poignant scene, Clooney's character asks a distraught employee who has just been fired how much money they had paid him when he started working to abandon his dreams. It wasn't much. Clooney's character then proceeds to help the employee rekindle his boyhood dream of becoming a chef and doing something that he and his grandchildren would be proud of.

How many people have worked for years in a work environment knowing that something was missing? Rather than being a labor of love, it was just labor. Maybe there had been a few incentives included along the way, but it was not the fulfilling vocation that had enthusiastically sparked early career choices.

If nothing else, we want you to take away insights from the book about how to enter your flow channel and we want you to accept responsibility to do so.

Throughout the chapters of this book, you have framed the context within which you work today and focused on developing the areas that are important to deliver your unique value. It is now necessary to ensure that the conditions are right for you to navigate within your flow channel to reach your full potential.

Of course, it is not just the exercises in this book that will make things happen for you. You will have to maintain a clear view of your vision and your purpose. This book, now your Journey Map, will help. However, healthy doses of passion and perseverance will be required along the way. It will take consistent effort and the rewards will be worth it.

Your vision

As you approach the end of this book, what is your vision for your future? Let's narrow it down. What is your vision of the future, two years from now? Imagine that all the problems have been solved and all the barriers have been overcome. You have entered your flow and are enjoying your success.

EXERCISE: Two years from now

Write down what this future looks like. What is happening around you? What are you doing? With whom are you doing it? How do you feel?

As you do this exercise, really try to imagine that you are two years in the future. Do not write about how it happened and what you had to do to achieve this future. Allow yourself the freedom to dream that it has already happened.

This concept of "future writing" can be incredibly powerful. Once you have written about what your ideal future looks and feels like, it can stimulate your thinking about how to bridge the gap between where you are now and where you would like to go.

From techie to author and back again

During a visioning workshop in Austria several years ago, participants were asked to carry out this exercise from a personal perspective. Bettina, a young, hard-working, and successful technology consultant, took the exercise seriously.

When she presented her vision, she explained earnestly that she wanted to write a book. At the time, Bettina's work and family commitments prevented her from writing it. However, as she dug deeper, Bettina realized that she had ignited, or rather re-ignited her true passion.

Several months after the workshop, Bettina took an unpaid sabbatical from work so that she could write her book. She was successful and managed to have it published. Since then, she has written several other books. Bettina went back to her technology career but with greater balance, less stress, and ultimately more personal satisfaction and success.

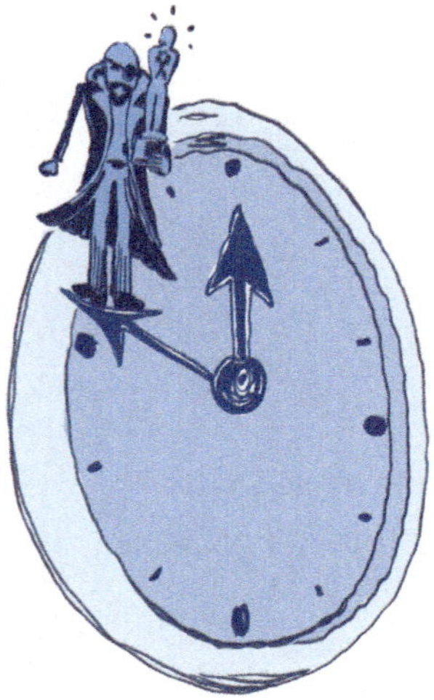

It's not too late

We often read about many personal endeavors where inspiring individuals have set some incredible goals for themselves, reaching great heights or performing death-defying feats when they were younger than we are now. However, there are many examples of people who have achieved personal success later in life.

Actor Samuel L. Jackson was forty-five when he had his big break in the film *Pulp Fiction*. Today, he is regarded as one of the most popular actors of his generation as well as being one of the highest-grossing actors of all time. Ray Kroc was a milkshake mixer salesman until, at the age of 55, he started to build the franchise model for McDonald's. The iconic painter Grandma Moses (Anna Mary Robertson Moses) didn't start painting until the age of 75. She only started painting when the arthritis in her hands prevented her from knitting.

Your personal vision and transformation agenda can begin at any age and do not have to impress others. They only have to impress you. It is your vision, your agenda. It might be directly in line with what you are currently doing and have done for many years. Or it might be something different, something that you have always wanted to do. Circumstances might have made you deviate from that destination, but the desire is still there.

Now you have the opportunity to rekindle that desire and take a fresh look at the possibilities to turn your vision into reality. Changing your current career path can deliver many benefits. However, too often, we follow the path of least resistance, the one that easily opens for us, from our academic achievements through to our career choices.

Significantly, however, it has been shown that early achievements in one domain do not necessarily translate into future success. Conversely, as with the examples above, the so-called "late bloomers" provide examples of individuals that have entered a new domain later in life, achieving considerable success and personal satisfaction.

The important thing is to take the time to review and refine your Journey Map on a regular basis. Taking time to realize that it is always possible to make changes, no matter where you are in your career or, indeed, your life.

Your actions will make the difference

The Irish playwright George Bernard Shaw wrote: "The reasonable man adapts himself to the world: the unreasonable one persists in trying to adapt the world to himself. Therefore, all progress depends on the unreasonable man."

You must be willing to be unreasonable to make change happen. To create the future that you want, every action that you take on your transformation journey must be aligned with the future desired state in mind.

Your actions will make a difference to you and to those around you. When you have a new spring in your step, when you are energized and operating in your flow channel, people will notice.

Baby steps

Mr. Wiggins was the wise, old, and grumpy math teacher that Paul had in the Fairfax High School for Boys. As he wandered around the classroom, glancing at the efforts of his students, he would often grunt and comment upon seeing someone's poor work, "Some people live and learn, and some people just live."

As you take action to make changes in your daily life and work environment, you must be willing to learn from your mistakes as well as from your successes. Being more observant of your own actions and the effect that these actions have on others is an important step. Also, paying more attention to the things taking place within your organization can help you to gain insights into the norms that have been established, and perhaps need to change.

We recommend that you take baby steps when you have decided to make change happen. As the English writer Alexander Pope wrote in *An Essay on Criticism*, "Fools rush in where angels fear to tread." His work advocates knowing one's own limits. He poetically says, "Launch not beyond your depth, but be discrete and mark that point where sense and dullness meet."

Far from being a timid approach to entering your flow, taking successful small steps requires setting realistic expectations for yourself. It is like building a fire; you start slowly with some kindling and a spark, eventually adding fuel to stoke the flames.

It will be necessary to evaluate the current state of your situation and to define your desired vision. You can then plan the transition or transformation realistically. Perhaps this will involve some deviations along the way to explore and experiment, but in doing so, the vision that you define for the future will guide your progress.

Identifying and overcoming obstacles

When you are enthusiastic about making a change, it can be tempting to ignore the obstacles that might exist. However, depending on their level of difficulty, these obstacles can slow you down or even prevent your progress. Let's look at four of them

Irritation

These are minor obstacles. You accept them as being a proverbial pain in the neck. Take, for example, a typical tedious company vacation planning system that requires you to struggle with a poorly designed system to enter your requested vacation dates. Or that weekly team meeting that is so mundane and repetitive that you cannot wait for it to end. These are the sorts of irritations that you can live with, and probably do. You accept them as the norm, tolerate the inconvenience, and carry on.

Labyrinth

Within any organization, processes and procedures can be long and cumbersome. Multiple stakeholders become involved, and decisions take time. For example, obtaining a budget for a new project can be a painstakingly long process. You typically know how to navigate the labyrinth, but it takes time and effort and a certain amount of determination to succeed.

Wall

When trying to achieve a goal, you can often come up against a wall, something that is blocking your path. For example, a company that has implemented a sales tracking system might mandate that all sales opportunities be entered into this system. Once this has been done, there is an automatic micro-tracking of the opportunity. Your intuition and experience as a sales specialist tell you that this is not the right way to track progress, but the system has become a wall. Not all walls are insurmountable. However, with a concerted effort, maybe a team effort, an obstacle that is perceived as a wall can be surmounted.

Chasm

The Grand Canyon in the United States is an example of a chasm with an enormous expanse of almost 5,000 square kilometers. A classic example of a chasm within corporations can be the love-hate relationships that often exist between different departments such as sales, marketing, finance, innovation, research, and development, etc. Each department has a perspective on their mission and the way things should be done. Finding a joint approach on how to work together can be a major challenge. Crossing a chasm can be daunting, however, with the right amount of effort, collaboration, and patience, it can be done.

EXERCISE: Obstacles

Think of the obstacles that you face in your working life today and how you want to proceed toward your vision for the future. Now, place them in the template below.

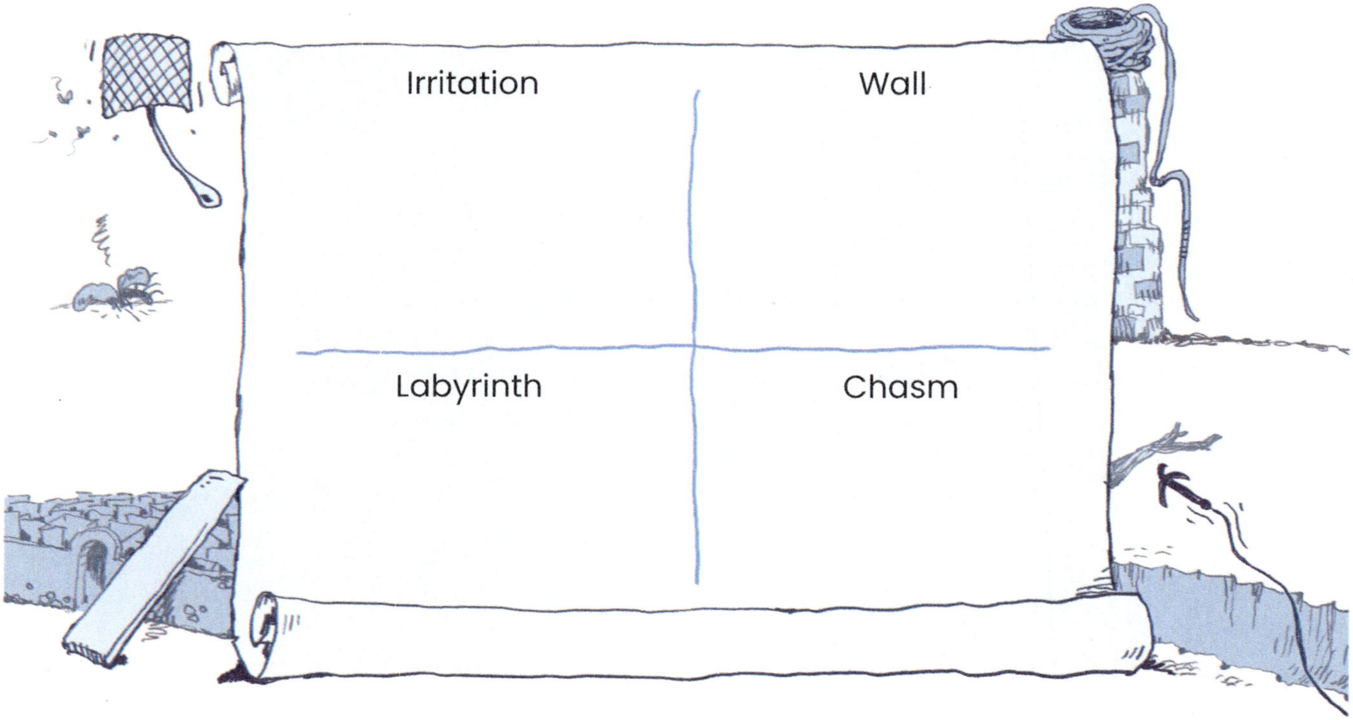

Each of the obstacles that you identify can inhibit or prevent your progress to reach the desired state of your future vision. Can you tolerate them? Can the obstacles be overcome? Must they be overcome? Depending upon your answers, the removal of an obstacle might become a project or personal campaign, in its own right.

Although it might seem like a deviation from the big changes that you want to make, by removing or limiting the impacts of the identified obstacle, you will not only simplify your life, but also enable more rapid progress to be made towards your goals.

One more thing: When evaluating these obstacles, be sure to spend some time thinking about whether you have any limiting beliefs about your ability to overcome any of them. If so, go back to the exercises on limiting beliefs in Chapter 4 and repeat them for the relevant obstacle.

From baby steps to bold steps

By taking the time to identify the obstacles and prioritizing how you will deal with them, you will have a clearer idea of the challenges ahead. Some things will be easy to accomplish. It might simply be to rearrange your day to ensure that you have some prime time to yourself. But what about those large obstacles that you have identified, the ones that seem like an impenetrable wall or a daunting chasm? How are you going to tackle those?

In his timeless Stoic work *Meditations*, the Roman Emperor Marcus Aurelius wrote, "The impediment to action advances action, what stands in the way becomes the way." In other words, your difficult challenges might very well be the place you need to start. Author (and modern Stoic) Ryan Holiday explores this idea in his book, *The Obstacle is the Way: The Ancient Art of Turning Trials to Triumph*.

Prioritization will be important when planning your way forward. Often, when you start to think about planning, you look to the future. You have a goal in mind, a future state, and you start to think about the steps that need to be taken going forward. Although this can sometimes work, typically what happens is that you start to do a deep dive on each step before having a clear picture of the roadmap that needs to be followed. There is a better way to plan that involves traveling to the future … and then looking back.

Dear Me ...

Above, we asked you to write down your vision and desired state two years from today. We now want you to put pen to paper one last time.

EXERCISE: A letter to yourself

Spend some time reviewing your Journey Map, all the things that you have discovered about yourself and the aspirations that you have defined. The last thing you should review is your vision of the future from the exercise a few pages above.

Once you have done so, we would like you to write a letter to yourself. Put today's date at the top of the letter and then begin, "Dear Me ...."

In this letter you are going to make a commitment to yourself. You are going to write about all the things that you will do to turn your vision into reality. This is an important letter, possibly the most important that you will ever write. The person to whom you are writing is counting on you to keep your commitments, so give it some deep thought.

Write about the changes you will make to turn your vision into reality. Write about strengths to improve, limiting beliefs to overcome, obstacles to surmount, and relationships to strengthen (or abandon). Your letter might include concrete plans for improvement as well as key milestones along your journey.

Please be specific about the things that you will do to reach your goal. The important thing is to have a clear idea of the key achievements that are necessary for you to arrive at your desired state.

Fold your "Dear Me" letter and your Vision document and put them away in a drawer. Now, schedule a regular time in your personal calendar when you will take them out, read them, and assess how you are doing. We recommend once a month, ideally on the same day every month so that you make it a habit. (You now know about the power of habits!)

Perhaps everything will be on track; perhaps you will need to adjust, perhaps you will need help with something. The key is to check regularly to ensure that you are on course.

GREETINGS
Dear me,
To

What now?

You have taken the time, not only to read about how to enter your flow channel, but also to reflect on your personal approach and attitude to your work life. However, as we have said a few times, thinking is not enough. The real challenge is to start implementing the changes that you want to make.

On page 261, you read the story about Bettina, the technology consultant who wanted to become an author. Her ambition created a disruptive change in her life. This disruption enabled her to rebalance her work, family, and life priorities. Not all changes have to be this disruptive. It will, however, be necessary to create a clear picture of the changes to be made and to recognize the results as their impact takes hold.

Do not place a value judgment on a change as to whether it is significant or not. Keep the big picture firmly in focus as multiple changes help to make the difference and the power and momentum starts to take hold.

Celebrate success, celebrate failure

The saying "Rome was not built in a day" reminds us that you are on a long and continuous journey. Many successes as well as failures will be encountered along the way. In almost all approaches to creating change, people tend to emphasize celebrating successes. This might be the success of a personal nature or maybe with the team within which you work. Recognizing and celebrating success is important. But what about your failures?

We are often told that we need to learn from our mistakes. Our parents and teachers probably reinforced this message many times. But why can we not also celebrate failure?

The desire might be to learn from a mistake and to quickly move on, perhaps not even mentioning it to anyone who did not notice. However, the world-renowned orchestral conductor Benjamin Zander has a different approach to failure. He tells his students to develop the attitude of expressing jubilant joy whenever they make a mistake, and then to learn from it. The joy comes from the learning that is possible *because* the mistake was made.

Some forward-thinking companies have even formalized this process. The idea is simple. Organized events enable employees to openly share mistakes that they have made, either individually or as a team. These mistakes might be anything from sending an email to the wrong address, to missing a deadline. People appreciate each other's honesty and support each other. The discussion is focused on how to improve in the future.

A Journey with No Sense of Distance

As you accept and launch yourself on your journey, it will be evident early on that it is a personal quest. There will be no teacher or guru watching your progress to give you your next colored belt at a grading ceremony. Although others might notice a change in you, the real feeling of progress will be up to you to interpret.

This is your journey, a journey of continuous discovery and fulfillment, a journey with no sense of distance but with a clear direction.

Although this might at first seem like a lonely path to take, there are myriad benefits from sharing your experiences and to learning from others. This is how we, the authors of this book, were fortuitously able to come together in 2020 and explore our individual experiences and insights.

When we set out to write this book, we had (and still have) a burning desire to share and help others discover the fulfillment and happiness that can be achieved in their work life. Although the core focus has been on your relationship with the work that you do, we hope that you also recognize the implications for your life outside of work.

We do not know what prompted you to read this book. However, if you have done the exercises and reflections along the way, this book is now different from when you picked it up. There will never be another book like the one you are holding in your hands. It has become a unique book about *you* and no one else. We hope that it has shed more light for you on who you are and what contribution you want to make to the world.

We encourage you to keep the book in a handy, nearby place so that you can refer to it easily. Come back to it from time to time and reflect on how your situation has evolved, where you have made progress, and where there is still work to do. Whether you need to work on connecting with others, finding your motivation, adjusting your aspirations, being more creative, communicating more effectively, or making good decisions, this book, now your Journey Map, will help you know and understand yourself better.

And, as the Greek philosopher Aristotle said, "Knowing yourself is the beginning of all wisdom."

About the authors

An accomplished coach and trainer with over 25 years of experience, **Tony Anagor** works with CEOs, leaders, and their teams to enhance emotional intelligence, communication, negotiation skills and handling challenging conversations. Of Nigerian heritage, born and raised in London, and now residing in Barcelona, Tony is passionate about personal growth and success strategies.

A native Hungarian now living in Paris, **Zsuzsanna Ferenczi** is a strategic advisor and mentor. She works with leaders from startups to Fortune 500 companies, helping them lean into their uniqueness so that they can express who they truly are and make the impact they are here to make. Zsuzsanna's 26-year journey leading highly engaged teams around the globe in the high tech and finance sectors has made her passionate about connecting at a deeper level with people from all cultures.

From early beginnings as an engineer and computer scientist, and through his work in research, teaching and consulting, **Paul Jeremaes** has always been passionate about the importance of creativity and innovation. As the founder and former director of the Hewlett-Packard EMEA Customer Innovation Centers, he helped organizations and individuals to create breakthrough business ideas and turn those ideas into a business success. Today, Paul, who comes from England and lives in Switzerland, continues to research and promote ways to democratize innovation in the workplace.

Raised in rural Illinois, **Kevin Woodson** has spent a lifetime helping people and organizations around the world find inspiration and collaborate on projects that make a difference. Kevin's repertoire includes graphic recording, fine art, and illustration. He regularly exhibits his paintings and sculpture, facilitates strategic visioning in businesses, and is art director of Living Lab Gallery in Taiwan, where he currently resides. Through his illustrations in this book, Kevin has brought together his individual skills and practices into a single work.

An expert in public speaking, **John Zimmer** comes from Canada and now lives in Switzerland. He practiced law for 25 years with a major Canadian law firm and the United Nations. John is passionate about the power of persuasive speaking. Today, he works with companies, organizations and individuals to help them articulate their ideas clearly and convincingly. John is also a member of an improv group in Geneva. Besides performing on stage, he helps people discover the many benefits of improv for their organizations.

For more information

If you would like to join our community, or if you would like more information, please visit us at www.worklife-flow.com or use the QR Code below.

Printed by Amazon Italia Logistica S.r.l.
Torrazza Piemonte (TO), Italy

45975996R00159